STUDIES IN
ANTHROPOLOGICAL METHOD

General Editors
GEORGE AND LOUISE SPINDLER
Stanford University

MANUAL FOR KINSHIP ANALYSIS

MANUAL FOR
KINSHIP ANALYSIS

ERNEST L. SCHUSKY

Southern Illinois University

HOLT, RINEHART AND WINSTON

New York   Chicago   San Francisco   Toronto   London

FOREWORD

About the Series

Anthropology has been, since the turn of the century, a significant influence shaping Western thought. It has brought into proper perspective the position of our culture as one of many, and has challenged universalistic and absolutistic assumptions and beliefs about the proper condition of man. Anthropology, the study of man, has been able to make this contribution mainly through its descriptive analyses of esoteric ways of life. Only in the last decades of anthropology's comparatively short existence as a science have anthropologists developed systematic theories about human behavior in its transcultural dimensions. Only still more recently have anthropological techniques of data collection and analysis become explicit and replicable.

Nearly every issue of every professional anthropological journal contains statements of methodological innovations. Our discipline is in a seminal period of development.

Teachers of anthropology have previously been handicapped by the lack of clear, authoritative statements of how anthropologists collect and analyze relevant data. The results of fieldwork are available to students in the ethnographer's published works. Although these demonstrate cultural diversity and integration, social control, religious behavior, marriage customs, and the like, clear, systematic statements about how the facts are gathered and interpreted are rare in the literature readily available to students. Without this information the alert "consumer" of anthropological results is left uninformed about the processes of our science—an unsatisfying state of affairs for both the student and the professor.

Our Studies in Anthropological Method series is designed to help relieve this tension. Each study in the series focuses on some manageable aspect of modern anthropological methodology. Each one demonstrates significant aspects of the processes of gathering, ordering, and interpreting data. The studies are written by professional anthropologists who have done fieldwork and who have made significant contributions to the science of man and his works. The authors explain how they go about this work, and to what end. We think the studies will be useful in courses ranging from the introductory to the graduate levels.

About the Author

Ernest L. Schusky is associate professor of anthropology and chairman of the behavioral science faculty at Southern Illinois University. His major interests are social structure, culture change, and applied anthropology. He completed his Ph.D. at the University of Chicago and has done fieldwork among the Papago, Iroquois, and Sioux Indians. He studied in India during the summer of 1964 as a Fulbright scholar. He has published on Pan Indianism, community planning, Dakota Sioux culture change and economic development. Dr. Schusky is a Fellow of the American Anthropological Association, the Society for Applied Anthropology, and the American Ethnological Association; he is an Associate of *Current Anthropology* and of the American Sociological Association.

About the Book

This book is about kinship. No subject occupies more space in professional journals, and perhaps none is as vexing to students. The study of kinship in its manifold systematic forms is of singular importance to anthropology because it is a dimension of behavior that is significant in all human societies and that can be made explicit and concrete by competent analysts. It is also a most complex dimension. Given our own rather unique "Eskimo" type of kinship system, Americans find it difficult to understand the divergent systems of kin ordering in other societies.

Dr. Schusky has given us a clear and simplified statement of some essential features of the study of kinship. He introduces concepts sequentially and logically, then demonstrates each step of his analysis. He observes good instructional techniques by providing exercises that build understanding as complexities unfold. And he refrains from introducing the more problematic developments in conception and analysis and directs his efforts at the basic essentials in procedure that must be mastered first. The result will be useful, we think, to many students and professors in general anthropology and intermediate level social organization courses.

GEORGE AND LOUISE SPINDLER
General Editors
Stanford, July 1965

CONTENTS

Introduction

THE STUDY OF KINSHIP is significant for modern anthropology in several ways. First, theories of human behavior have been tested by kinship analysis. For instance, much has been learned about the relationship between the beliefs or ideal behavior of a people and their actual behavior by study of kinship practices. Second, particular kinship practices are useful in making historical reconstructions. Third, understanding of kinship behavior is invaluable for the anthropologist in field work. Among many peoples kinship is the basis for most behavior and the anthropologist quickly makes sense of why people interact in the way they do once he understands their kinship system. Finally, analysis of the meaning of kinship terms has led to new understandings of how people view the world or at least how they make classifications of parts of it.

Kinship was studied by early anthropologists as well as those of today. Initial interest centered on showing how various social practices evolved. The "evolution" of family life received particular attention, and Lewis H. Morgan concentrated on the whole range of kinship. Morgan (1870) partially lost sight of human behavior because of his enthusiasm for terminology; he also exaggerated the importance of kinship terms in reconstructing history. However, he collected terminology for so many tribes that his work is still used and some of his conclusions have been the germ for much of current theory. Another anthropologist of this period, W. H. R. Rivers, is also responsible for stimulating present kinship analysis.

In the early 1900s anthropologists attacked the approach of social evolution and turned to the historical method. Much time was spent simply in criticizing the social evolutionists, and when kinship was studied, it was for the purpose of establishing historical contacts between peoples. Items of kinship terminology were reported, but historical anthropology failed to see kinship *systems.* However, some notable anthropologists of the period managed to keep a systematic analysis of kinship alive. A. L. Kroeber and Robert Lowie, especially, looked for correlations between kinship and other areas of behavior. Their contribution to scientific analysis of kinship and their roles in shaping theory is explained by Sol Tax (1955b: 467–477).

The groundwork for modern theory about kinship and much of social science began about 1920 with the development of functional anthropology. Two English anthropologists, Bronislaw Malinowski and A. R. Radcliffe-Brown, are largely responsible for changing anthropological perspective. Malinowski's

1

descriptions of kin behavior were thorough and his emphasis on behavior rather than terminology led to many developments. First, theorists saw more clearly the relations between kinship and other institutions and, second, description of behavior pointed up the systematic behavior involved in kinship. Although Malinowski was a pioneer in both functional anthropology and intensive field work, his description and analysis were of such caliber that they are still frequently used. (See paragraph M 4 below.) Although Radcliffe-Brown differed with Malinowski on a number of theoretical issues, he too saw kinship as a system. His generalizations about kin behavior in certain social contexts has stimulated numerous studies (Radcliffe-Brown and Ford 1950) and demonstrated the extent to which the methods of natural science can be followed in the social sciences.

In current anthropology the study of kinship is of primary importance for its use in theory. Gibbs (1964) points out that this theory has been "matrix-centered" and "kinship-centered." In the former, economic, political or other practices are used to explain kinship behavior. The latter explains one aspect of kinship in terms of another; and generalizations about types of descent and residence practice can be quite precise. Principles, comparable in precision to those in physics, have not been discovered but much regular, recurrent behavior has been discovered. Murdock (1949), for instance, formulated a general "postulate" of kinship behavior from which he derives a number of "theorems." The theorems illustrate one way in which social science can predict or formulate "laws" of behavior. Kinship studies have also been valuable for functional theory; they show very well how parts of culture are interrelated. In any discussion of kinship some mention must be made of religion, politics, economics, or other facets of culture. It is simply impossible to describe kinship behavior without reference to almost every other aspect of culture. It becomes quite clear that different culture complexes are but part of an over-all pattern. Recent emphasis on changing kinship systems may well offer insights into the processes which operate to form the over-all pattern.

Kinship also may serve as a model or map of human behavior. If an anthropologist knows only the kinship terminology of a people, he is equipped with many expectations and can appropriately anticipate and understand behavior. Thus, a knowledge of kinship is invaluable for the field work of the cultural anthropologist. Moreover, most kinship practices are readily discussed by informants, so an initial task of a field worker is to record how people are related to each other.

The importance of kinship may be illustrated by an anecdote many anthropologists tell their students about Australian aborigines. When two aborigines meet the first thing they do is discover how they are related. Until they know their proper relationship, it is not possible for them even to exchange greetings. When aborigines first met Europeans, no bond of kinship could be established. As a result the aborigines attempted to kill whites because such action was the only conceivable behavior to take with a nonrelative. The truth of the story is less important than the value of the illustration that kinship is central in the lives of many people. Not only are the rules of behavior toward kin extensive; one finds that almost everyone he interacts with is some kind of relative. In field work the anthropologist frequently hears from community members, "We are all relatives here."

Finally, kinship is important in theories of cognition. Anthropologists may study terminology for the purpose of semantic analysis. In this process, the meaning of terms is discovered by looking at how relatives are grouped. The way in which classes of relatives are perceived, as revealed by analysis of component parts, gives insight into how people view their relatives. It may reveal also principles of classification by which other parts of the world are divided. Goodenough (1951; 1956b) and Lounsbury (1956) drew attention to componential analysis. Further evaluation of the technique was supplied by Wallace and Atkins (1960) while Pospisil and Laughlin (1963), Landar (1962), and Burling (1963) published componential analyses of particular groups. The field is yet too young to be thoroughly evaluated, but Burling (1964) raises some serious questions of methodology. A most extensive review of the field has been offered by Lévi-Strauss (1963). He points up the need for a method in kinship study analogous in form to the method used in structural linguistics.

Although the importance of kinship for all the new theory cannot be detailed here, it should be obvious that a thorough grounding in kinship is valuable for an understanding of cultural anthropology. Most anthropology textbooks have not been able to devote adequate space for the study of kinship. Hopefully, this manual will fill the gap. It consists of a series of exercises designed to give an introductory student a grounding in the various classifications of kinship systems; it also introduces most of the concepts and parts of social structure that traditionally have been closely associated with kinship. This method of study has been found most useful for introducing basic concepts; students generally can learn the material with only limited guidance from the instructor. For advanced problems in kinship, three dimensional models seem essential. Edward A. Kennard has experimented with such models and will supply information to interested instructors; he may be reached through the Anthropology Department of the University of Pittsburgh.

Part One

A. Elements of Kinship

1. A basic building block of kinship in most systems is the *nuclear family,* or parents and their children. The organization of this family may differ considerably from the American model; the couple may live in the household of the wife's mother, the children may be disciplined by other than parents, or economic support may be provided by the wife. Although behavior differs widely, the structure of most kinship systems begins with the nuclear family.

2. This family necessitates two kinds of kinship relations. The parents are tied by a marital bond, one the anthropologist calls *affinal.* In addition to his wife the husband also finds he is now related to his wife's parents, her brothers and sisters, and many others. Parents are related to their children in a different type of relation. It is commonly known as a blood relation but the anthropologist refers to it as a *consanguineal* relation. In short, the nuclear family is composed of *affinal* (marital) and *consanguine* (blood) ties of kinship. Generally, the affinal ties are of a contractual nature and can be broken. The consanguine ties, on the other hand, are a matter of birth and are irrevocable.

3. A third possibility of kinship ties is *fictive.* In our own society adopted children or godchildren are made "relatives" by establishment of a "fictitious" kin relationship. The custom of other people in making "blood brothers" is well known, and in Latin America godparents are generally quite important relatives. Deshon (1963), for instance, describes the importance of godparents and their relation to each other in a particular Latin community.

B. Diagraming Kinship Ties

1. In analyzing kinship behavior it becomes necessary to turn to diagrams. In some societies one regards a mother's brother as quite a different relative from a father's brother. The mother's brother may be the person to whom ego is indebted for his future possessions and position. The father's brother, however, may be considered as an altogether different kind of relative and is of no importance in a man's economic or social life.

Americans, of course, think of both men in the same category and call both "Uncle." This example illustrates the necessity for precision in designating relationship. Analysis of kinship soon leads to talk of a mother's mother's brother's daughter's daughter. At this point one must concentrate hard and usually mumble aloud, "My mother's—mother's—brother's—daughter's daughter." A diagram simplifies understanding of the relationship.

2. Think of the factors that must be involved in diagraming the above relationship. Sex is obviously one, generations another and finally affinal ties must be distinguished from consanguine ones. The sex symbols of the biologist, ♂ and ♀, have been found inconvenient. Therefore, a triangle is used for male, a circle for female. One line indicates a consanguine relation, two parallel lines an affinal relation. Generation can be indicated by relative position with children placed below parents.

△ male   = marital or affinal tie

○ female   — consanguine tie

Exercise 1. Use these symbols to diagram a nuclear family of father, mother, brother, and sister. Label the symbols "father," "mother," "brother," "sister."

3. Your diagram should look like this:

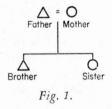

Fig. 1.

Or is this diagram correct? What would be incorrect about the following diagram?

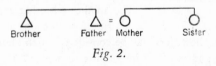

Fig. 2.

The male on the far left is a "brother" to the male labeled "father" and the woman on the far right is a "sister" to the female labeled "mother." Precision in terminology can be introduced, however, by naming the relatives from the viewpoint of one individual. This point is elementary and must be thoroughly understood! In order to avoid confusion, the system must be entered at one point and viewed only from that point. To indicate the point, one of the symbols, usually an adult male, is labeled EGO or the symbol may be darkened. In the following diagram, then, there is no confusion over terms. The man labeled father may be a brother, as well as a father, but this is irrelevant if the system is viewed only through ego's eyes.

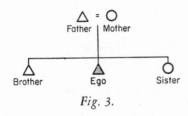

Fig. 3.

4. Assuming that ego is an adult male, he is likely to be married. In America he will generally start his own, independent nuclear family. Socially he becomes a member of a second family. Everywhere man is faced with the fact that he is a member of two nuclear families and this fact raises certain problems. For instance, where is the new family to reside? What roles will a person have in each of the families? How does an individual move from one family to the other? Many solutions have been devised for these problems but men everywhere have something in common because of their membership in two families.

5. The ego of Figure 3 is involved in a family that for him consists entirely of consanguine kin: his parents and his brothers and sisters. (The brothers and sisters are called *siblings*. This term is simply a shorthand device like the word "parents.") For ego it is the family in which he learns his culture or is oriented toward adult life. It is called a family of *orientation*.

6. Once ego is "oriented" he may begin a family of his own. One of his primary duties in this family is the procreation of children. This family is called one of *procreation*. The *affinal* tie of spouse is highly important but *consanguine* ties to children are also important.

Exercise 2. Construct a diagram showing both ego's family of orientation and procreation. Draw a solid line around the family of orientation; draw a broken line around the family of procreation.

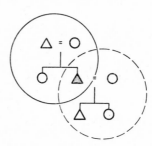

Fig. 4. Correct diagram for Exercise 2 should resemble this one.

C. Abbreviations in Kinship

1. Kinship diagrams must often be small in order to be printed or simply in order to be convenient. Therefore, it is often impossible to spell out fully the appropriate terms in English. Moreover, long combinations of terms are frequently used in a text and abbreviations of terms are further necessitated. For instance, something like the following "language" appears in an article in the *American Anthropologist* (Matthews 1959). Surprisingly, it takes only a little practice to read this esoteric tongue. In the Hidatsa language, *ate* = FaPaSbSo, FaMoBr, FaSiSo, FaSiDaSo; in the Mandan language *at* = FaSiSo (with a suffix), PaFa, PaPaFa, HuFa, FaSiHu, FaSiDaHu, FaSiDaHuHu. . . .

2. In most cases the abbreviations are simply the first two letters of the word abbreviated. Fa = father, Mo = mother, Si = sister, Br = brother, So = son, Sb = sibling (because Si is used for sister). These terms are simple and will cause little confusion. However, it probably will take practice to recognize immediately that Pa = parents, Hu = husband, Wi = wife, Ch = child, Sp = spouse, La = in-law. Once used, the abbreviations save so much time and space they become invaluable both for study and for use in field work.

3. One should be warned that the above abbreviations do not exhaust all possibilities. In some societies a man may call his MoBr by one term

while his Si uses a completely different term for the same person. Such a practice sounds odd (and somewhat discouraging) at first, but Americans are familiar with it. A woman is likely to call her father "daddy" but a man would hardly think of addressing his father in such a way. Thus, it may be necessary to indicate whether a male or female is speaking before appropriate kin terms can be supplied for a diagram. To complicate the matter further, some societies have no term for brother; rather, they specify whether the "brother" is older or younger than ego and have separate terms for the two categories. Appropriate abbreviations for such a situation usually will be supplied in the description. It must be emphasized that such differences must be noted, not for the sake of precision, but because differences in terms may be a clue to differences in behavior which are not readily observable. Terminology is generally an index of behavior and it is behavior which is of interest to the anthropologist.

4. A word of warning will conclude this discussion of abbreviations. The system described here has not been standardized and the student may run into other kinds of designations. For instance, "S" might be used for "sister"; "s" for "son." English anthropologists frequently use "Z" for sister; "S" for son.

Exercise 3. Label the following diagram with appropriate abbreviations. (*Note:* Disregard English terms such as "uncle"; specify the relationship exactly: FaBr rather than "uncle." For reasons to become apparent later, it is often necessary to think in terms of a FaSiSoDa rather than cousin. The preceding exercise should help in developing such thinking.

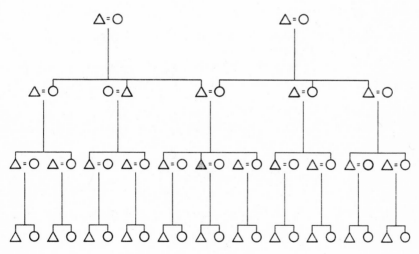

Ex. 3. Diagram for Exercise 3.

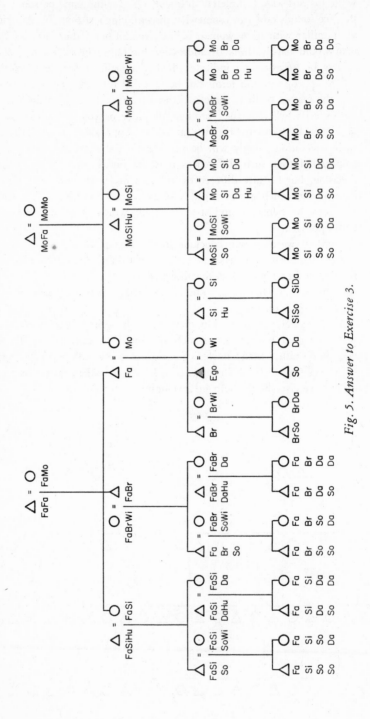

Fig. 5. Answer to Exercise 3.

D. American Kinship

1. The kinship terminology of Exercise 3 emphasizes exact relationship. Its contrast with the American system appears below. In the following exercise write in the terms, such as "uncle" or "cousin" which you would use in referring to these relatives. Note that a number of possible relationships have been dropped for the sake of simplicity.

Exercise 4. Write the English term you would use if you were ego.

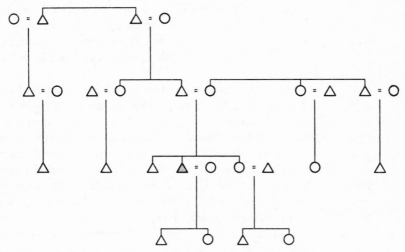

Ex. 4. Diagram for Exercise 4.

2. It is impossible to supply a "correct" answer for this exercise. Americans, like other people, have variation in their terminology. As noted before, a male will probably have one kinship term for "father" while a female may use some other term. Moreover, not much is known about American kinship terminology. Anthropologists have been remiss in studying most parts of their own culture; one of the few studies of American terminology (Schneider and Homans 1955) raises as many questions as it answers.

3. Further, Fa may have been labeled "father," "dad," or "pop." Or Mo may be labeled "mother" "mom," or "ma." The main difference in terms

is whether ego is talking *to* or *about* his relatives. In other words, one is likely to talk to another about his "father," but one will say "Dad, can I have the car tonight?" In the first instance, in *referring* to a father, a *term of reference* is used. In the second case, a *term of address* has been used. In doing research it is important to determine both terms of address and terms of reference. In anthropological reports *terms of reference* are most often the ones used for analysis.

4. A difficulty often encountered in the exercise is the labeling of ego's FaFaBr. People who have such a relative may immediately think of him as a "great-uncle," but others might not use such a term. However, the real confusion begins with FaFaBrSo. Is he a "cousin," "first cousin," or a "cousin once removed"? What is ego's FaFaBrSoSo? Is he a "cousin once removed," or a "second cousin"? There is no standard answer because Americans do not agree on the definition of these terms. In some societies, however, a man would regard FaFaBrSoSo as a brother, and call him by the same term as his male sibling. Americans tend to deny any relationship to such a person by failing to agree on any term. Instead, they lump many such "strangers" into one category—"kissing cousins." The point to remember is this: Some people recognize consanguine or affinal relationships as "close" which other people regard as "distant" or may even ignore.

5. Study of the American diagram can tell us some other important things about kinship everywhere. For instance, what are the full meanings of each of the terms? What does "aunt" denote? First, it specifies sex; second, it specifies generation. "Aunt" is a woman in my mother's generation or, as anthropologists say, "a female in the first ascending generation." Furthermore, the term indicates she is a female parental sibling or the spouse of a male parental sibling. Almost all American terms specify not only the sex of a relative but whether he or she is in the same, first ascending or first descending generation. In fact, by using the prefix "great" Americans can specify *any* number of generations. Anthropologists have found that all over the world societies have divided work and other activity along age and sex lines; therefore, it is not surprising that kinship systems seldom fail to denote with exactitude the generation and sex of a relative. Generation is such an important factor in determining kinship terminology that it is known as the *generation principle*. Likewise, anthropologists refer to a *sex principle*.

Question: What is the one American kinship term that does not specify sex?

6. Study of American kinship further helps in understanding another division of kin that most systems make. Note that direct descendants, ego's Fa, FaFa, FaMo, Mo, MoFa, MoMo, So, Da, GrSo, and GrDa are all differentiated from their consanguine relatives in each generation. Those persons who are all in the same line are known technically as *lineal* relatives. The relatives not in the line are called *collateral* relatives. In the first ascending generation all collaterals are lumped in the categories uncle and aunt; in the second ascending generation, great-uncle or great-aunt. In ego's generation all cousins are collaterals. Brothers may or may not be considered collaterals. A discussion of their anomalous position is beyond the scope of discussion here.

7. Finally, American terminology illustrates one of the most important aspects of kinship study. The terms reveal much about general behavior. For instance, Schneider and Homans' analysis (1955:1199) of American kinship terms for uncle and aunt suggests a subordination of women to men and a possibility that women display less affect than men. A study of terminology does not usually *prove* any such features but the work illustrates how terminology may reflect much on behavior outside kinship.

Exercise 5. Darken the lineal relatives in the following diagram.

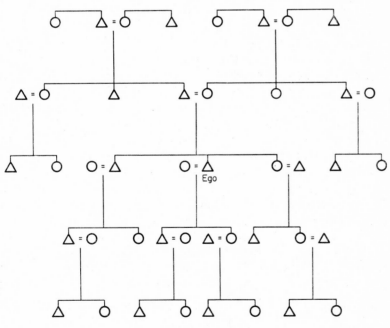

Ex. 5. Diagram for Exercise 5.

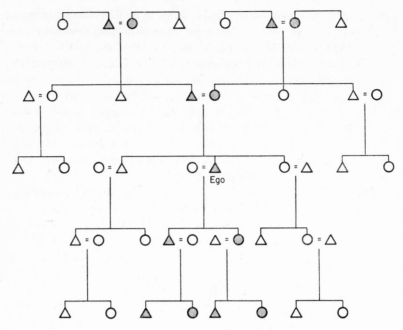

Fig. 6. Answer to Exercise 5.

E. Other Kinship Systems

1. Americans take their method of recognizing kin so much for granted that students generally find it difficult to realize that other peoples operate on entirely different assumptions in the recognition of relatives. Everywhere children begin learning their kinship system as soon as they learn to speak; therefore, it is no wonder that everyone takes his kinship system for granted. In the study of kinship one's first impression is that man has devised an endless variety of relationships, but the really remarkable fact about kinship is that of all the logical possibilities, man has selected only a few.

2. In most of Polynesia and in many other places around the world, *lineal* ,relatives are not differentiated from *collateral* ones. Only the principles of sex and generation operate. That is, there is one term for each of the males in ego's generation and one term for males in each of the first and second ascending and descending generations. Such a system is sometimes called *generational*. The system can be understood best by studying Figure 7.

3. One of the first things asked about such a system is, Do they really think they have two or three mothers? What must be understood is that the word interpreted as "mother" does not have the same connotations as it

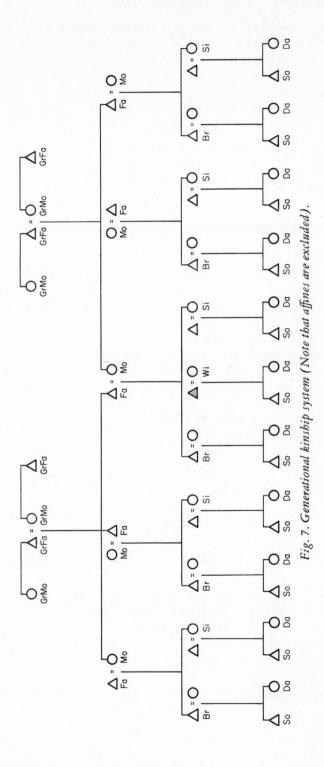

Fig. 7. Generational kinship system (Note that affines are excluded).

does in English. The term in a Hawaiian system emphasizes the social role of motherhood and minimizes the biological role. That is, all the women called "mother" act very much in the same way toward ego. Although individuals do know their "real" mother, the biological fact is simply not very important. Lowie (1948:64) concisely describes the behavior associated with Hawaiian terminology.

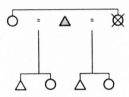

Fig. 8. The sororate.

4. Early anthropologists, such as Morgan (1870), explained the Hawaiian and other systems largely on the basis of hypothetical marriage practices. Such an analysis is now considered inadequate, but the explanation was simple. It is useful today to introduce a discussion of kinship, and it helps students to keep in mind why certain kinds of relatives are grouped together under the same term. An easily understood marriage practice is the *sororate,* in which a man is expected to marry the sister of his deceased wife. The sororate is diagramed in Figure 8; X denotes the death of ego's first wife. The *levirate* is a similar marriage custom. This practice requires that a widow marry the brother of her deceased husband. The levirate is diagramed in Figure 9.

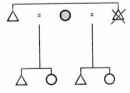

Fig. 9. The levirate.

An examination of the sororate in practice points up why more than one woman might be considered a "mother." When ego's father marries his wife's sister in Polynesia, he is marrying someone ego already calls "mother." Thus, ego may be partially alleviated of the adjustment an American child must make when he acquires a new mother, a woman who is only qualifiably a "mother." Even in terminology she becomes only a "stepmother." The structure of the levirate is similar. Ego's mother remarries someone ego already calls "father" in a generational system.

5. Because Americans are so grounded in their own kinship system, a ques-

tion of availability invariably arises: What if a man's wife doesn't have any sisters or they are already married? Remember that in a generational system all of ego's cousins are his siblings. In Figure 7 ego's wife could marry not just ego's immediate brother but anyone ego calls brother. Remember the diagram is an ideal type and is limited just to show possibilities; even so, there are five "brothers" available to ego's wife should ego die. Moreover, the levirate and sororate are usually forms of *preferential* marriage. Such a marriage is the ideal or desired form, but if it is not practical, then alternatives are available. The living spouse may marry anyone, or through some social fiction a proper "brother" or "sister" may be created. However, the levirate and the sororate may occur as *prescribed* forms; in such a case no alternative is allowed a widow or widower and if no eligible sibling is available, remarriage is impossible.

6. In America a man occasionally may marry his wife's sister. Such a marriage is not termed a sororate. What is important is *expectation* or *ideal*. That is, a society is said to practice the sororate when there are rules or norms that specify such a marriage. Or we might say that the practice is *institutionalized;* it is a way of doing something.

7. A word of caution about the sororate and levirate must be added. It is known now that these practices do not explain adequately generational or other types of kinship. However, such an explanation does enable one to understand and remember better the organization involved in different kinship systems.

F. Kinship Classifications

1. In general, kinship systems may be divided into two groups, generational and lineal, but the use of such a broad classification is limited.

2. One of the first classification systems was proposed by Lewis Henry Morgan, a pioneer in the study of kinship. His system is like the one described above. Morgan calls *descriptive* the system that clearly distinguishes lineal from collateral relatives. A *classificatory* system is one that lumps some or all collaterals with lineal relatives. Morgan contributed so much to kinship analysis that his scheme is often used and is classic. However, classification has been much refined. The system detailed below is currently the one most often used by anthropologists.

3. Today kinship systems are classified most often by the way in which ego addresses his cousins. The American system, comparatively rare among all the cultures of the world, is called *Eskimo*. The system introduced above, where all cousins are equated with brother and sister, is called *Hawaiian*. As mentioned before, it is found in most of Polynesia, but it also occurs in many places around the world. The other types of kinship systems are known as *Iroquois, Sudanese, Crow,* and *Omaha*. Descriptions of these will be given later.

G. Cousin Relations

1. The explanation of the sororate or levirate as preparation for ego to call someone mother or father is much too simple; moreover, it is far from adequate. Ego's FaSi could not possibly become FaWi. This man and this woman are siblings and incest rules would prevent their marriage. However, the marriage customs are useful for understanding why ego's FaBr might be a "father" and why ego's MoSi might be a "mother." This pair of relations is so frequently classified with ego's parents that it is useful to designate them. Anthropologists call them the parallel aunt and uncle. That is, FaBr and MoSi are the parallel uncles and aunts.

2. Kinship systems, unless undergoing change, are consistent. I will call "brother" anyone who is a son of my father; the children of my mother will be my brothers and sisters; thus, the children of parallel uncles and aunts are my brothers and sisters whenever FaBr = Fa and MoSi = Mo.

    Anthropologists designate such kin with a technical term—*parallel cousins.*

Exercise 6. Draw a diagram showing parallel cousins.

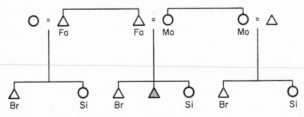

Fig. 10. Exercise 6 should resemble this diagram; one often finds the attached labels.

(*Note:* The wife of FaBr is a woman married to my "father"; often such a woman becomes "mother." Similarly the Hu of MoSi becomes Fa, but remember that affinal terminology is not so consistent as consanguine terminology. FaBrWi may be a descriptive term literally translated as "Father's Brother's Wife.")

3. We are now left with the relatives, MoBr and FaSi. These are the people that many societies think of as "uncle" and "aunt." The anthropologist, for convenience, calls these the *cross-uncle* and *cross-aunt*. Their children become *cross-cousins*. That is, ego's MoSi's and FaBr's children are *parallel cousins;* his FaSi's and MoBr's children are *cross-cousins*. A more succinct definition is this: Children of siblings of the same sex are parallel cousins; children of siblings of the opposite sex are cross-cousins.

Exercise 7. Draw a diagram showing ego's parallel and cross-cousins. Indicate cross-cousins by an "X"; parallel cousins by "//". The X and // are symbols used by anthropologists.

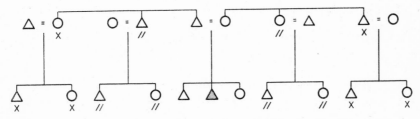

Fig. 11. Correct diagram for Exercise 7 should resemble this one.

If we were to label the diagram of Figure 11, lumping // cousins with siblings but differentiating cross-cousins, we would have what is known as the Iroquois type of kinship. It is convenient to draw diagrams so that the cross-cousins are located on the extreme left and right of ego. Then the grouping of parallel cousins with siblings is emphasized.

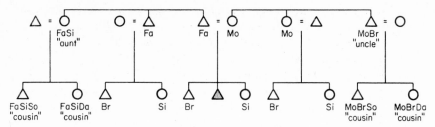

Fig. 12. Iroquois type of kinship terminology.

H. Review

1. Three types of kinship systems—Eskimo, Hawaiian, and Iroquois—have been introduced. These can be identified according to the way in which *cousins* are treated. *In the Eskimo system all cousins are equated and differentiated from siblings. In the Iroquois system sibling terms are extended to parallel cousins; there are separate terms for cross-cousins. In the Hawaiian system sibling terms are extended to all cousins.*

   Figure 12 diagrams Iroquois terminology. Hawaiian and Eskimo systems are summarized by Figures 13 and 14.

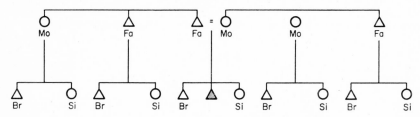

Fig. 13. Diagram of Hawaiian terminology.

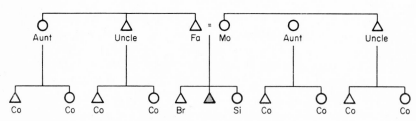

Fig. 14. Diagram of Eskimo terminology.

2. All these systems are balanced. That is, the terms on the mother's side are essentially the same as those on the father's side. Such terminology is an indication that kinship is bilateral. However, Iroquois terms frequently appear among groups that are not bilateral. Ego is likely to in-

herit an occupation, group membership, property, or prestige from either or both parents. Most importantly, descent is traced through both sexes. It is most useful to remember this point—in bilateral systems descent is through *both sexes.*

3. American kinship is an example of bilaterality. In tracing ancestry both the mother's and father's lines usually are given equivalent treatment. Inheritance rules, which usually but not always parallel descent rules, generally require that both sexes receive equal treatment. For instance, American parents distribute their property among their children irrespective of sex and usually the division is fairly equal. Moreover, all children inherit the parents' social class initially although they may change class later in life.

4. Inheritance rules are usually indicative of how people relate to each other through generations, but it is also important to determine the rules for linking persons of different generations. These rules of descent may vary from norms of inheritance. For example, with the isolation and independence of the contemporary American family, it is difficult to appreciate how much emphasis other people have placed on descent rules. Bohannan (1963:127) describes how Anglo-Saxons in medieval times were obligated to sixth cousins. Imagine how many of both mother's and father's ancestors must be remembered. At some point, however, relationships had to be severed. All kinship systems face the problem of excluding some relatives while including others. The Anglo-Saxon group excluded collaterals beyond sixth cousins by including only a certain number of generations. Most other peoples have solved the "exclusion problem" by including only relatives who have a common ancestor and who can trace ascent to that person entirely through one sex. When ascent is through males, or *ancestors,* the group is said to be *agnatic;* where ascent is through females, or *ancestresses,* the group is *uterine.* In either case what emerges in kinship is one line or a *unilineal descent group.* Such a system is difficult for Americans to comprehend. Relatives on the mother's side are of a different type from those on the father's side. The idea of descent itself is quite different from our own, where we think of mothers and fathers each contributing one half to our life. Trobriand Islanders, for instance, deny any real importance to the male in the procreation of children; as one would expect, descent is through females and this linkage is emphasized by biological belief. Obviously, doctrines of procreation are of much importance in the field of kinship; Bohannan (1963:133–136) illustrates how beliefs about conception among a number of unilineal peoples correlate with their descent rules.

I. Unilineal Descent

1. In order to develop a "feeling" for unilineal systems imagine a hypothetical society of hunters and gatherers where men hunt and women

gather. A man teaches his son hunting techniques in a hunting territory. Possibly the man has certain privileges in this territory. Meanwhile, the mother is teaching her daughter the techniques of gathering; possibly she has certain rights regarding berry patches or nut trees. Each activity contributes about one half to the total subsistence. What happens when the children become adults and marry? Will a man inherit and stay in his father's hunting territory and bring a wife who must compete with his sister? Or will the man leave and let his sister's husband occupy the hunting territory? It is quite possible that no rules will be institution-alized. Either the brother or the sister may stay and inheritance does not become fixed in one sex.

2. Contrast these hunters and gatherers with their hypothetical neighbors who are horticulturalists. Here the women spend most of their time with the domestic crops. Men do some clearing and some harvesting, but women take the major interest in the fields. Daughters inherit their mother's fields and their knowledge of agriculture. Women may provide 80 or 90 percent of the subsistence. Mothers have a vested interest in the important factor of land. They could pass on their land to their sons' wives, but the daughters are already familiar with the land. Assume they choose their daughters. Sons must go to live with their wives who are inheriting land from their mothers. The society practices what is known as matrilocal residence. A household consists of a woman, her daughters, their daughters, and any unmarried sons. All of these are consanguine relatives. The husbands of these women are in the house-hold through affinal ties; possibly none of the men are related to each other. One must study this situation to appreciate fully the positions of men and women. An adult male marries and moves into a household occupied by his wife, her mother, her sisters, and her unmarried brothers. Most other adult males in the household are in the same position as he is—a virtual stranger. If trouble occurs with the wife, the man has a host of consanguine relatives allied against him. For solace he must remain tied to his mother's household and his own lineage; the situation re-

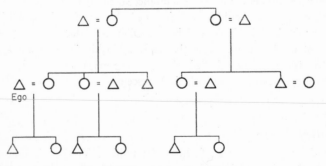

Ex. 8. Diagram for Exercise 8.

emphasizes the importance of the female line. Ego's position may be understood better by completing Exercise 8. Concise descriptions of family life in such circumstances are provided by Malinowski (1960:233–238) and Barnett (1960).

Exercise 8. Ego is in a matrilocal household. Darken all the consanguine relatives of ego's wife. Note that all these relations, except one, will be in the household ego is to occupy. Which relative is the exception?

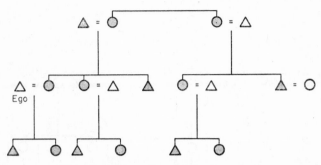

Fig. 15. Correct diagram for Exercise 8.

Ego's WiMoSiSo will not be in the household. He has moved into the household of the line of women his wife represents.

J. The Lineage

1. The hypothetical horticulturalists have kinship groups called *lineages*. A line of females and their brothers forms a group with enduring relations. The lineage owns property, perhaps has certain of its own rituals, and members have rights and obligations toward one another because of lineage membership. Just how a lineage system develops is not entirely certain; the system is much more complex than the simple transmission of property or rights as described above. The salient feature of the lineage is that it has rights, ritual, or property *as a group.* Americans are unfamiliar with such activity in kinship, but do recognize it as corporate behavior. The parallel between the lineage and the modern corporation will be spelled out later. It may be noted here that lineages seem to occur in societies which acquire certain kinds of wealth and pass on this wealth to heirs in particular ways. Lineage development seems especially appropriate in societies where wealth must be controlled by one sex or the other.

2. The lineage, of course, unites many people over generations. It may even incorporate a dead ancestor, as in ancestor worship, and take into account members in a generation yet to be born. Very large numbers of people can be united through lineage organization. On the other hand, the lineage acts as a dividing force within society. Alliance and responsibility

to the lineage may interfere with duties toward spouse or age mates or even tribe. Moreover, lineages often come to compete with each other. Although lineage bonds are generally strong, the possibility of splintering is inherent in lineage organization. Possible separation of the group occurs whenever there are two or more siblings of the same sex through which descent is traced. Consider what might happen to a *line* of women when a mother has several daughters, as in Figure 16. In four genera-

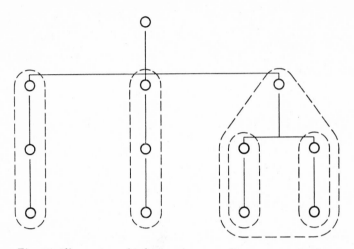

Fig. 16. Illustration of inherent danger to lineage organization.

tions three "lines" have appeared and even a fourth may possibly develop. If the female who originated this lineage should be forgotten, then the tie between the three lines is lost and there are now three divisions or lineages.

3. The three lineages can be kept whole, however, by replacing the "forgotten" ancestress by a mythological ancestress. Anyone then tracing his ancestry to a common source, even if it is mythical, is related in lineage fashion. People all over the world have worked out such a development. Technically, this kind of grouping is known as a *sib*. (British anthropologists and a number of Americans use the word *clan* instead. The glossary at the end of the text provides a guide for which words different anthropologists have chosen.)

4. Remembering that the sib has created its unity by replacing a lost ancestor with a mythical one enables us to understand the structure of the sib. However, this explanation is only an aid to memory; it has been found inadequate as a full explanation of sib development.

5. Sib membership, like lineage membership, is traced through *one* line, either male or female. A system which follows the male line is called *patrilineal;* one which follows the female is called *matrilineal*. Do not think of patrilineal as "father's line"; think of it as a male line. Similarly,

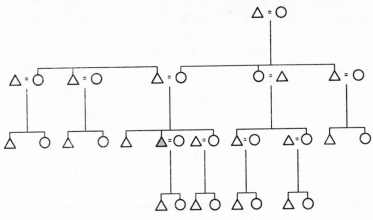

Ex. 9. Diagram for Exercise 9.

the matrilineal line is a female line. Anthropologists frequently speak of *agnatic,* rather than patrilineal, relatives; or *uterine,* instead of matrilineal, relatives to stress the point that descent is through one sex rather than through one of the parents.

Exercise 9. Ego is in a matrilineal society. Place a dot in all the relatives in ego's sib.

6. Note that the children of ego are *not* in his sib. However, the children of ego's sister are in the same sib as ego. What property, obligations, or privileges ego has *as a sib member* cannot be passed on to his own children. His logical male heir is, instead, his sister's son. Or considering ego as an heir, he cannot look to his father but rather he looks to his mother's brother. Let us return to the hypothetical case of horticulturalists. Ma-

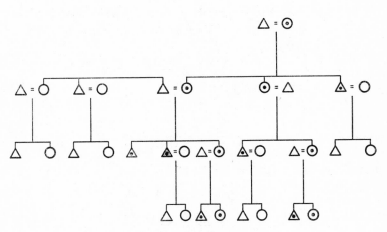

Fig. 17. Correct diagram for Exercise 9.

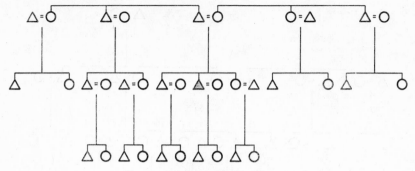

Ex. 10. Diagram for Exercise 10.

trilineal lineages were combined to form matrisibs; descent is through women. However, men retain or develop ritual appropriate to their sibs and hold sib offices. Their knowledge or position must be taught to a younger generation. The man's own son has been born into a different sib; therefore, the father's knowledge or power is inappropriate. But the man's sister's son is of his sib and becomes a logical heir. Everywhere in societies with matrisibs, the mother's brother–sister's son relationship is most important and the MoBr in some ways resembles the father in a bilateral or patrilineal society. The study of this relationship has recently been summarized by Lévi-Strauss (1963:40–51), whose analysis is most stimulating.

7. The principles of patrilineal organization are much like those of matriliny. Thus, an introduction to patriliny will serve as a review of the former. In the following exercise note that descent is exclusively through males but that the resulting organization is similar, though reversed, to that diagramed in Exercise 9.

Exercise 10. Ego is in a patrilineal sib. Place a dot in all the relatives in ego's sib.

Note that in both systems males and females are included, but in a patrilineal system descent *ends* in females; in a matrilineal system descent *ends* in males.

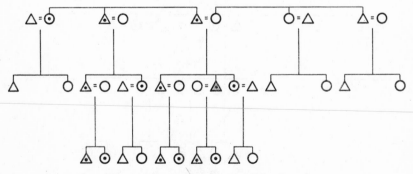

Fig. 18. Correct diagram for Exercise 10.

K. Lineage and Sib Characteristics

1. All relations within a sib or lineage are consanguine. In one way, the relationships may be considered to resemble the sibling tie, and lineage and sib mates will behave toward each other accordingly. Therefore, one does not marry a sib mate; the relationship is considered to be much too close. Thus, lineages and sibs are generally *exogamous*. That is, members must marry *outside* their sib or lineage. (*Endogamy* is marriage within a group.) This rule means that most or all in-laws are automatically of another sib or lineage.

2. In the sib the mythical ancestor of the patrisib or ancestress of the matrisib often becomes a super or nonhuman figure. Quite often animals or plants are the mythical founders of a sib, but such phenomena as rain or clouds may also be designated as having sib origins. Whatever the symbol, it is known as a *totem,* an Ojibway Indian word meaning "the symbol of a sib." Sibs everywhere usually have a totem, but sib organization is occasionally found without totems. Occasionally, groups other than sibs possess totems. Early anthropologists made exhaustive studies of totemism, but with only a few exceptions (Lévi-Strauss 1962) the subject has received little attention in modern anthropology.

3. The lineage and sib may also have characteristics of *corporate* groups. The usefulness of the concept of corporacy for sib analysis lies in its emphasis on the *perpetuity* of a group regardless of particular members. Just as the General Electric Corporation will outlive the lives of all its membership today, the sib continues after the death of any particular member. Besides this characteristic of perpetuity, the corporate group has property (nonmaterial as well as material), a name, often a symbol such a totem or the GE trademark, rules of membership, and often special norms. However, unlike the modern corporation whose shareholders are strangers to each other, the members of a lineage or sib have close emotional ties.

4. The primary point to remember is that a sib is highly important for the individual in a unilineal society. The sib may determine for the individual whom he can marry, his occupation, his religious role, and his place in the prestige system. The sib, in a way, constitutes a society within a society.

L. Kinship Systems in Unilineal Societies

1. To understand Crow and Omaha kinship types, so often found in unilineal systems, the nature of sib organization must be clear. It is useful to summarize: (1) Sib members, in one sense, *are thought of* as brothers and sisters; (2) ego belongs to only *one* sib—usually the one in which

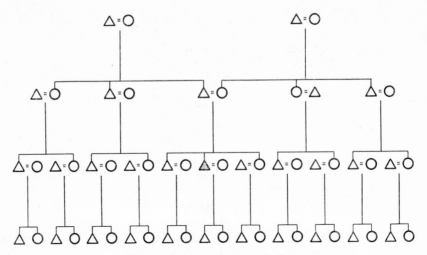

Ex. 11. Diagram for Exercise 11.

he is born although an exceptional sib may have achieved membership; (3) still, ego is bound by a parental tie to another sib. That is, ego will feel a special tie to his father's sib if in a matrilineage or to his mother's sib if in a patrilineage. Eggan (1950:111–116) provides a concise analysis of matrilineal behavior among the Hopi. The following exercise will clarify ego's relation to the sibs.

Exercise 11. Ego is in a matrilineage. Place a dot in his sib relations. Place an X in the sib relations of his father.

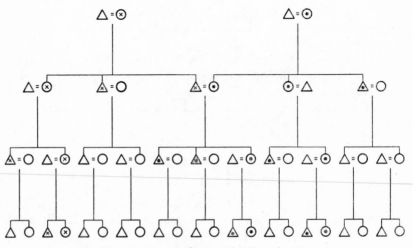

Fig. 19. Correct diagram for Exercise 11.

2. With the characteristics of the sib in mind, let us start with the basic kinship system of Figure 10, where parallel cousins are equated with siblings and FaBr = Fa, MoSi = Mo. In a unilineal system, we should expect that the cross-uncle and the cross-aunt will be quite different kinds of relatives to ego. One belongs to ego's sib; the other does not (see Figure 19).

3. Imagine the life of ego in Figure 19. He is to grow up in his mother's sib. He must learn the male duties and prerogatives of his sib from his MoBr, *not* from his Fa. In turn he must pass on his learning to his sister's son, *not* to his own son. Either in the role of teacher or in the role of student the differences in age between sib members are important and

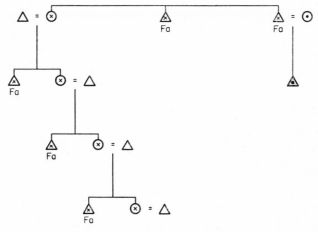

Fig. 20. The sib brothers of father who become "fathers" of ego in a matrilineal system.

age differences will be indicated by terminology. However, ego only infrequently interacts with his father's sib mates, and his relations here are not patterned subordination or superordination. In his *father's* sib it is possible to think of all sib mates of father as *brother* and *sister* to father. Ego's logic is: "Anyone who is a sib brother to my father is a brother to my father." What are FaBr called? Remember FaBr = Fa. It follows logically, then, that ego addresses a large number of people as "father"; what is even more striking to the person accustomed to bilaterality is that "father" may be of the same generation as ego or *even a generation below ego.*

4. The system is so unusual to a bilateral "thinker" that the accounts of early European explorers who encountered such kinship make amusing reading. A French explorer among the Illinois Indians decided the savages were so stupid they could not remember kinship terms and were likely to call anyone "mother," even small babies who "could not possibly be their mothers." Of course, once the principles of unilineal systems are understood, the terminology becomes perfectly logical.

5. The same principle of sib brothers becoming a "father" applies to women in father's sib. However, FaSi—the cross-aunt—is not a "mother" of ego. For convenience let us label her simply FaSi. Recall ego's view: "Any sib sister to my father is a 'sister' to my father." Therefore, all women in ego's father's sib become FaSi. Occasionally, all these women may be equated as FaMo rather than FaSi. The principle remains the same but does allow for variation in terminology.

Exercise 12. Label the following diagram in which sib mates become brothers and sisters of ego's father.

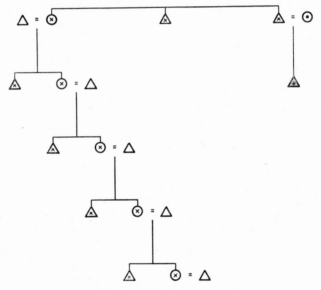

Ex. 12. Diagram for Exercise 12.

6. Note that a line of women, circled by the broken line, stands out in this *matrilineal* society. However, the line of women is on ego's *father's* side. Review paragraphs J 5 and 6 if you do not fully understand why the *female* line shows so clearly on ego's father's side.

7. Recall that two principles in kinship have been offered—the principle of generation and the principle of sex. A third, the *sib principle,* may now be added. In the system above, it could be said that the sib principle "overrides" the age principle. People of different generations are equated because they belong to the same sib.

8. With a knowledge of the father's side in this system, the mother's side can be figured logically because of consistency of kinship systems. In other words, there is a set of rules in kinship terminology which are nearly universal. Sol Tax (1955a:19–23) lists twelve such rules. Two of these are of immediate relevance.

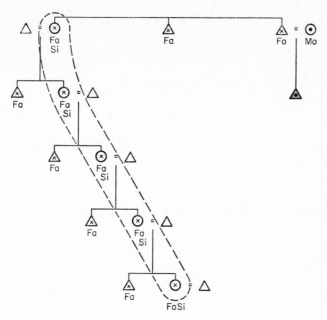

Fig. 21. Correct diagram for Exercise 12.

    a. The rule of uniform descent: If somebody whom ego calls A has children whom ego calls B, then the children of everybody whom ego calls A are called B.

    b. The rule of uniform reciprocals: If A and B are terms used between a pair of relatives, then the reciprocal of every A must be B.

Rule 1 is illustrated by American terminology for aunts. If somebody whom ego calls "aunt" (e.g., MoSi) has children whom ego calls "cousin," then the children of everybody whom ego calls "aunt" (e.g., FaSi) are called "cousin." Rule 2 is illustrated by aunt-nephew terms. Anyone whom ego calls "aunt" will call him "nephew," i.e., if aunt and nephew are terms used between a pair of relatives, then the reciprocal of every aunt must be nephew. Every kin term has a reciprocal, but the reciprocal may vary according to sex. The reciprocal of aunt is either nephew or niece, depending on the sex of ego.

9. With these rules in mind consider the relatives of ego on his mother's side in a matrilineage. Can you determine what a male ego's MoBrSo will be called? To work the problem consider the reciprocal relation between ego and *his* FaSiSo. He calls FaSiSo "father"; therefore, that man will call him "son." That is, anyone I call "father" will call me "son." Now think of yourself as ego's MoBrSo. What will you call Ego? _____ _____. If you call him that, what will he call you? _____. The missing term is

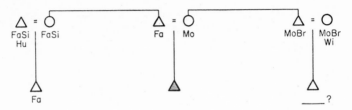

"son." Consider ego's relation to his FaSiSo. He is calling him "father" because this cousin is a sib mate of ego's father. Now recall the rule of uniform reciprocals. Anyone I call "father" will call me "son." Therefore, ego's FaSiSo calls ego "son." What is the relationship here? A MoBrSo should be a son also. Think of the missing position in relation to ego. Ego is someone in the sib of MoBr; therefore, he is a sib brother, therefore, a "father." Anyone who calls him "father," he will call "son." Again keep the two rules of reciprocity in mind and supply the missing terms for the children of ego's siblings.

Exercise 13. Fill in the terms for ego's sibling's children.

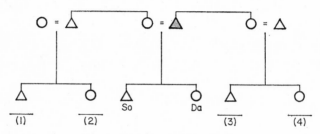

Ex. 13. Diagram for Exercise 13.

It is helpful to put yourself in each of the positions as you attempt to label them. What does 1 call ego? Ego, then, is a FaBr. FaBr = Fa. If 1 is calling ego "father," then ego will call him "son." A sister of a son is a daughter, so 2 becomes "daughter." The male in position 3 is in the relationship to ego of MoBr. The rule of reciprocity applies; anyone I call MoBr will call me SiSo (or nephew). Thus, 3 and 4 should be labeled SiSo and SiDa or nephew and niece.

M. The Crow Kinship System

1. The matrilineal system so far described is known technically as a Crow type of kinship system. The terms already worked out are the only ones needed to identify immediately the kinship system as Crow. The structure so far covered is presented in Figure 22. Note well the line of women

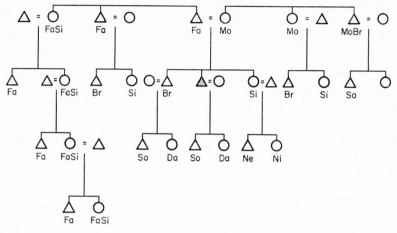

Fig. 22. Basic Crow system.

descended from FaSi; all of the line is equated as FaSi. Remember that they could also be FaMo; see paragraph L 5.

2. The terminology for a number of other relationships also can be determined logically. In the following exercise ask, "What are the children of such and such called?" That is, if ego addresses someone as father, then that person's children will be brothers and sisters of ego. The principles that provide the answers to the exercise follow it.

Exercise 14. Supply the missing terms in the nine spaces on the next page.

The logic to be used in filling in the blank spaces in Exercise 14 is this:

1 = Br because he is the son of a Fa. Rule 1 says "If anyone whom ego calls A (father) has children whom ego calls B (brother), then the children of everybody whom ego calls A are called B."

2 = So because he is the son of a Br. Read the rule again, substituting Br for Fa, A, and son for Br, B.

3 = nephew because he is the So of a Si. Rule 1 again explains the terminology. Sons of sisters are nephews.

4 = So for the same reason that 2 = So.

5 = Da; siblings of a So are So and Da.

6 = nephew for the same reason that 3 is a nephew.

7 = So because he is the So of a Br. Note that 7 is in the same position as 2 although 7 is a generation below 2.

8 = Br because he is the So of a Fa. Note that 8 is equated with

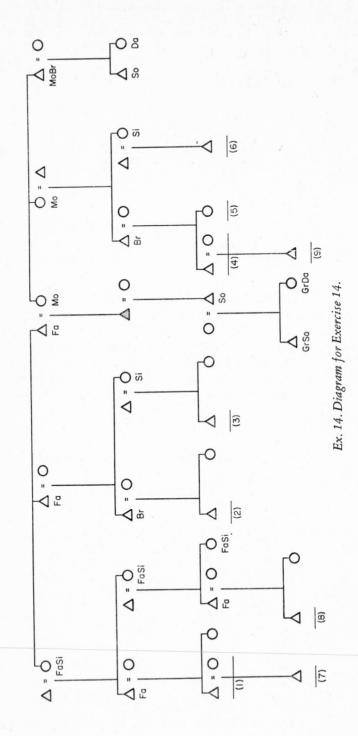

Ex. 14. Diagram for Exercise 14.

ego's FaBrSo, *two* generations above. This emphasizes that the word interpreted in English as Br certainly does not have the same connotations.

9 = GrSo because he is the So of a So. "If anyone whom ego calls A (son) has children whom ego calls B (grandson), then the children of everybody whom ego calls A are called B."

3. Study of Exercise 14 shows that the second ascending and second descending generations reflect differences in generation. That is, the principle of generation is again important. However, the principle of sibship still overrides generation in the line of females represented by FaSi, and the especially perceptive informant in a Crow kinship system will extend logically the line of FaSi to infinity.

4. The structure of kinship systems follows a logic that allows for an understanding of a system as complex as Crow terminology. The terminology, however, offers only the skeleton of the structure. To make the structure whole, the "flesh" of behavior must be added. A brief description of how one such Crow system works in everyday life may emphasize that anthropology's perspective must always be one of behavior; it is most important not to get so entangled in the maze of terminology that one neglects to notice how relatives interact with each other. A brief description of behavior patterns shown by a few Trobriander relatives illustrates the essentials of a Crow system. Remember, ego has one kind of tie to his mother's group; another kind of tie to his father's. His relation to his mother is different from his relation to his father; the MoBr–SiSo relation is of a particular nature.

A brief description of Trobriander family life appears in Goldschmidt (1960:233–239); Fathauer (1961) offers a detailed but concise analysis of Trobriander kinship and social structures. The relations between ego and his Fa, MoBr, and Mo are paraphrased here. Because the Trobriander ignores the man's role in begetting children, the word for "father" has only a social definition. It means "a man married to my mother." The "father" is often described as a stranger or outsider. Like the American father, the Trobriander is responsible for much of the care of the children and lavishes much affection on them. Unlike the American boy, however, the Trobriander, as he matures finds he belongs to a quite different group from that of his father. He also learns many duties, restrictions, and concerns for pride that unite him to his mother but necessarily separate him from father.

The separation from father is brought about largely by the emerging importance of the MoBr. The child finds that he is a "stranger" in the village of his father; his "own village" is that of his MoBr. There he

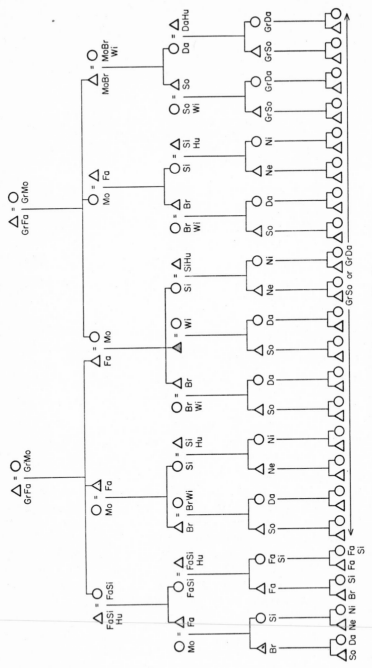

Fig. 23. Diagram of a Crow kinship system.

has property and other rights, a future career, and natural allies and associates. His MoBr increases authority over him, demands certain services of him, and grants or withholds permission over particular actions. The authority and counsel of the father decrease correspondingly.

Perhaps the greatest difference between a Trobriander and ourselves is the link between mother and child. Recall the Trobriander belief that a mother contributes everything to the makeup of the child. From the belief stem the rules of inheritance, succession in rank, chieftainship, and magic. A man passes his position to his sister's son and this matrilineal conception regulates marriage and restricts sex. The ideas of kinship are especially important at death. The norms specifying burial, mourning, distribution of food at the death feast and other ritual are all based on the principle that matrilineal relatives form a special, closely knit group. The group is so tightly bound by common feelings and interests that even those united to it by marriage and by a father-to-child relation are sharply excluded in many ways.

N. The Omaha Kinship System

1. The Omaha kinship system is almost a mirror image of the Crow kinship system. It follows the same logic except that descent lines are traced through males rather than through females. The following exercises, therefore, are repetitive but generally are quite useful for a thorough understanding of both Omaha and Crow systems.

2. For a "feeling" of the system let us return to our hypothetical hunters and gatherers. Assume that males perfect new hunting techniques which bind them to their territory and allow them to contribute most to the economy. Furthermore, the new techniques require the cooperation of several adult men. Two brothers and their sons make a logical cooperating team; at marriage the sons are persuaded to continue working with their fathers. Residence becomes patrilocal; unrelated females are now married to a line of males related by consanguine ties. This *patrilineage* (or line of males) assumes the characteristics of a corporate group in the same way as the matrilineage does. The lineages may well become grouped into sibs.

3. Kinship terminology reflects new behavior toward kin with the appearance of sibs. In Exercise 15, place a dot in members of ego's sib, an X in the sib mates of his mother. The parallel cousins, uncles, and aunts will be Br, Si, Fa, and Mo. Label them. Now recall ego's position with respect to his cross-cousins. His *matrilateral* cross-cousins (MoBrSo and MoBrDa) are not his sib mates but he recognizes MoBrSo as a sib *brother* of his mother and MoBrDa as a sib *sister* of his mother. What

are brothers and sisters of Mo called? ———————————————
———————. Now label the patrilateral cross-cousins (FaSiSo and FaSiDa).
The term will be the reciprocal of what ego calls his MoBrSo. That is,
ego is to MoBrSo what FaSiSo is to ego. Review of L 9 will provide
further clues.

Exercise 15. Label the parallel and cross-uncles, -aunts and -cousins in an
Omaha System

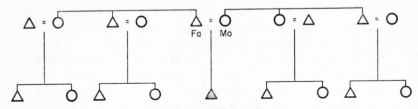

Ex. 15. Diagram for Exercise 15.

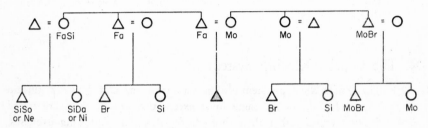

Fig. 24. Correct diagram for Exercise 15.

4. Before going further with the Omaha system, a problem of sex must be
interjected. Compare Figure 24 with Figure 25. The MoBr children in

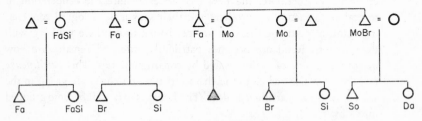

Fig. 25. Cross-cousin terminology in a Crow system.

Crow = son and daughter. If the Omaha system is a mirror image of
Crow, then in Omaha FaSi children should = son and daughter. But
Fig 23 shows that father's sister's children = nephew and niece. Note
what happens, however, when the female cross-cousin, MoBrDa, is considered rather than MoBrSo. If MoBrDa is a "mother," then ego be-

comes "son." Reciprocally then, FaSiDa becomes a "daughter." Brothers of a daughter become "sons." Whether the MoBrSo or the MoBrDa becomes ego's reference point usually depends on the sex of ego. Thus, a *female* speaker in an Omaha system may report a kinship system that

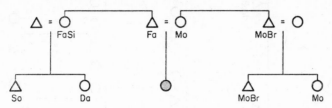

Fig. 26. Omaha system, female speaking.

is a true mirror image of a Crow system, *male* speaking. This example suffices to illustrate the necessity of gathering kinship terms from both males and females in a society.

5. To return to the Omaha system, complete the following exercise. Keep in mind the rules of uniform descent and the rule of uniform reciprocals. If you need further aid restudy the details of the Crow system, keeping in mind that the Omaha type is a "reflection" of Crow.

Exercise 16. Complete the labeling of an Omaha system on the next page.

6. For a further understanding of Omaha terminology, it is useful to see how the principles apply in actual behavior. The Bunyoro provide an interesting example; Beattie (1960:48–60) has described concisely the relations between kin. His description, here paraphrased, also points up one view of why Omaha terms are what they are.

The Nyoro people are patrilineal, and an individual inherits his sib (totem) membership in a particular kin group and most of his property from his father. At one time all the men of a sib lived together, but now sibs are somewhat scattered. The sibs are exogamous and ideally patrilocal, but a number of factors other than descent now determine residence. Agnates, or patrilineal kinship, are still important, however, in fixing personal loyalties, marriage, and inheritance; support and devotion among agnates are high. Thus, brothers reside near their fathers and keep close relations. This kind of *group* membership, Beattie stresses, and the social relations within the group greatly influence Nyoro thought about consanguine and affinal relatives and kinship terminology.

Nyoro terminology classifies some collateral relatives with linear relatives. A FaBr is called Fa, his So is called Br. A FaSi is called by a term that might be translated "female father." One's patrilateral relatives are all a kind of "sibling," "fathers" (male and female), or children. To call them such means to behave toward them, at least to some extent, as one

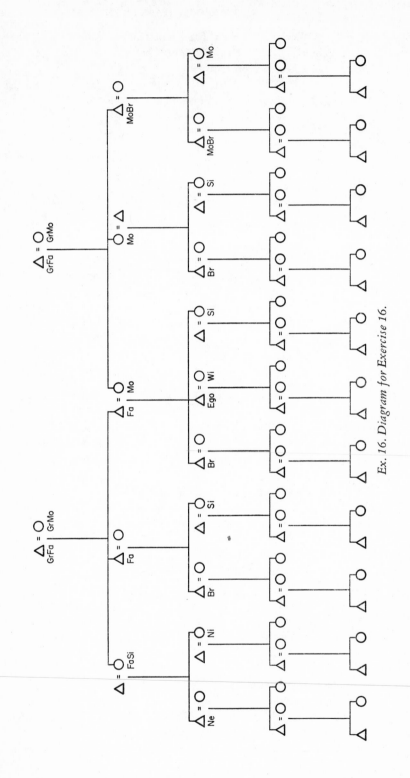

Ex. 16. Diagram for Exercise 16.

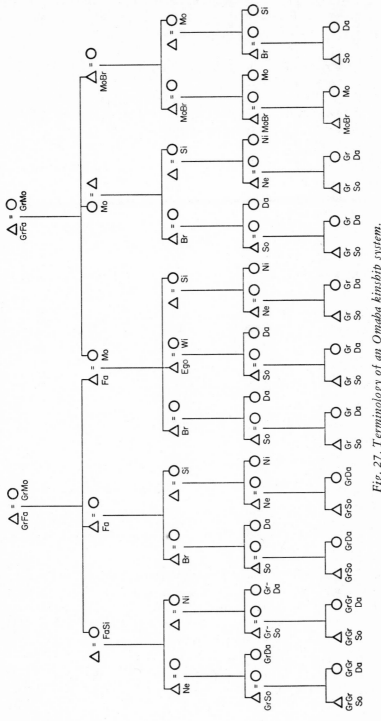

Fig. 27. Terminology of an Omaha kinship system.

does toward the nearest agnatic relatives. This usage extends to all persons within the sib, regardless of degree of relationship; and Nyoro consider it impolite to inquire about exact relationship between sib mates.

Relatives on the mother's side are also grouped together. MoSi is a kind of mother and her children are ego's siblings. The MoBr is a kind of "mother" and is called a "male mother." The practice seems strange, but remember that he is a member of the same lineage as mother. In a sense all the members of mother's agnatic group are "mothers."

The important principle is that members of one's own lineage are one kind of relative; members of mother's group are another kind of relative. Although Americans think of MoBr and FaBr as the same kind of relative and call both "uncle," the Nyoro see the two men as entirely different kinds of people. FaBr "belongs" to ego's important group; MoBr is "only" a member of mother's lineage. A Nyoro's expectations and obligations toward members of these two distinct groups are quite different.

A Nyoro is able to place almost anyone he meets in one of a few categories and immediately knows how he stands in relation to that person. If he meets a member of his own sib, that person is a father, brother, or son, depending on relative generation. Men of other sibs may belong to mother's group, in which case they become a kind of "mother," or of FaMo sib and therefore a kind of "grandmother," or of wife's sib and therefore a kind of brother-in-law. The sib system, combined with the classificatory principle, allows a few simple kin categories to be extended over a wide social field.

This system of kinship, which lends itself so well to Omaha terminology, consists of certain behavior between relatives. To contrast it with Crow organization, the relations between ego and his Fa, MoBr, and Mo will be described. (For review, see paragraph M 4, which covers these relationships for the Trobriander.)

A Nyoro father may have genuine affection for his son but the authority of fathers and the subordination of sons are always stressed. Fathers are addressed as "sir" or "master"; deference must be shown; and a man squats on the floor in the presence of his father rather than sits on a chair. Fathers determine for sons a proper spouse and when to begin shaving and smoking. The relation is marked by a latent hostility between the two. Beattie states that the son's rise to adulthood constitutes a challenge to the father and that a father resents his son's maturing because it threatens his own preeminence.

The relation to MoBr is much like that of a Trobriander for his father. Recall that MoBr was called a "male mother." This term is extended to MoBrSo and to the children of MoBrSo, which is the main characteristic of Omaha terminology. These relatives are all members of mother's agnatic descent group and so are thought of as "mothers." A Nyoro thinks of himself as a child of the whole agnatic group and his kinship terms and behavior are based on this view. All the relatives he calls "mother" are expected to be loving and indulgent. The "male mothers" are much the same as "mothers" and a sister's son is much freer with his MoBr's property than with his father's. He may borrow clothing, take food, and joke familiarly with MoBr. Nyoro often recount their happy visits to the homes of their maternal uncles.

Before he goes on to section O, it is most useful for the student to think of Trobriander and Nyoro behavior and determine for himself how this behavior accommodates itself so readily to Crow and Omaha kinship terminology.

O. The Causes of Crow and Omaha Terminology

1. Anthropologists are particularly interested in Crow and Omaha types, perhaps because they differ so much from the anthropologists' own kinship systems. Of prime importance, however, is that Crow and Omaha override the generation principle and indicate that some *sociological* institutions are part of kinship. A high correlation of patrilineal sibs with Omaha types and matrilineal sibs with Crow types is sufficient proof of the importance of a sociological cause. However, there are patrisibs without Omaha terminology and matrisibs without Crow terminology. Also, some societies may have Crow or Omaha terminology but lack sibs. In other words, sibs or other forms of social organization cannot be considered *the* causes of kinship.

2. One of the earliest explanations of terminology was diffusion or borrowing. Peoples next to each other generally have similar systems, and a *culture area* is frequently described by one system. However, in some areas all kinds of kinship systems exist side by side. Simple distribution analysis makes it look as if each group might have *independently invented* its own kinship system.

3. The "unexplainable" distribution of kinship types led 'some anthropologists to argue that a particular kinship system could only be understood through its *history.* That is, a group of people had a particular system because of certain historical events. Other anthropologists, using the same evidence, argued that some natural law must account for the similarities between systems widely separated and with different histories.

4. Sol Tax (1955a) clarifies much of this confusion in an analysis of an

area with diverse kinship. He points out that one is only misled by
by arguing on a basis of:

a. Sociological versus psychological factors
b. Diffusion versus independent invention
c. History versus natural law

Actually, all factors may be important and the task of the anthropologist
is to identify the contribution of each. Another danger in explaining
the "causes" of the kinship types is noted by Tax (1955a:13–14):

> . . . if clans (sibs) and/or the peculiar marriage have brought into
> being the Omaha or Crow types, then what brought the clans and
> the marriage into being? Is it actually more reasonable to suppose
> that the social institutions, rather than the kinship classification,
> came first?

5. Recent anthropological theory regarding Crow and Omaha types (cf.
Moore 1963; Lane and Lane 1959) is beyond the scope of this book.
In order to comprehend kinship systems so different from our own,
simple monocausal explanations were provided in the previous pages.
Section O, however, should provide sufficient warning that many factors
are responsible for kinship. More advanced work in anthropology will
provide a much better understanding of these factors (cf. Murdock
1949), but such work is only possible after one fully comprehends types
of classifications.

P. Review of Classification of Kinship Types

1. In the first three types of kinship, cousins on the mother's side are treated
in much the same way as cousins on the father's side. In the Eskimo
system FaBr and FaSi children are all cousins; on the mother's side MoSi
and MoBr children are all cousins. The Hawaiian system equates all cousins with siblings. In the Iroquois system the parallel cousins are usually
equated with siblings; cross-cousins are called by the same term but are
always differentiated from parallel cousins.
2. Crow and Omaha systems are usually, but not always found in unilineal
societies. In the Crow system, generally found in matrilineal organization, the FaSiSo = Fa, FaSiDa = FaSi; on mother's side MoBrSo = So,
MoBrDa = Da. Parallel cousins are siblings. In the Omaha system
FaSiSo = Ne, FaSiDa = Ni; MoBrSo = MoBr, MoBrDa = Mo. Parallel
cousins are siblings.
3. A sixth type of cousin classification occasionally found deserves brief
introduction. It has been labeled Sudanese and occurs over a wide area
in Africa and occasionally in other parts of the world. Each of the cousins
is given a distinct term and separated from siblings. In other words, the
system describes the cousins' relationship to ego precisely.

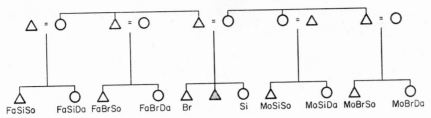

Fig. 28. Sudanese type of kinship.

4. The classification reviewed here is based on terms for *cousins*. It is the most widely used taxonomy in kinship studies, but another kind of classification may be used to emphasize other aspects of kin behavior.

Q. Classification by First Ascending Generation

1. Only the basic essence of this classification scheme is to be presented here. For a full discussion of the taxonomy refer to Lowie (1948).
2. Only the females in the first ascending generation need be considered to understand the implications of this type of classification. Thus, three relatives are involved: mother, mother's sister, and father's sister.
3. Some people, including ourselves, designate mother with one term and lump MoSi and FaSi under another term. This system is called *lineal*.
4. In a *generational* system all three women are equated. Recall the Hawaiian system where all women a generation above ego are labeled "mother."
5. In the Iroquois system recall that mother's sister became a mother, but

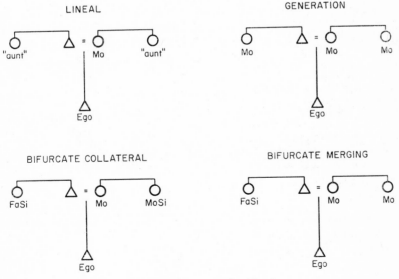

Fig. 29. Mother-aunt classifications.

father's sister did not. This terminology is known as *bifurcate merging*. Most Crow and Omaha systems, like Iroquois, are bifurcate merging.

6. In some societies, especially with Sudanese cousin terms, each woman in the first ascending generation has a separate term. This practice is labeled *bifurcate collateral*. Bifurcate collateral terminology emphasizes the two forks of ego's ancestry and separates lineal from collateral relatives. Bifurcate merging distinguishes both ancestral lines but merges Mo and MoSi on the one fork. Figure 29 illustrates the different ways in which Mo, MoSi, and FaSi may be lumped or separated.

R. Review

1. At the conclusion of this part you should be equipped with the basic vocabulary involved in the study of kinship. Write out definitions for the following list of terms. Your answers may be checked with the glossary.
   consanguine
   affinal
   fictive
   family of orientation
   family of procreation
   term of reference
   term of address
   lineal relatives
   sororate
   levirate
   parallel cousins
   cross-cousins
   patrilineal
   bilateral
   avunculocal
   neolocal
   endogamy
   exogamy

2. You should also be capable of classifying kinship systems on the basis of terminology. Classify the following systems first by cousin-type terms, then by first ascending generation. Answers are provided at the end of the section.

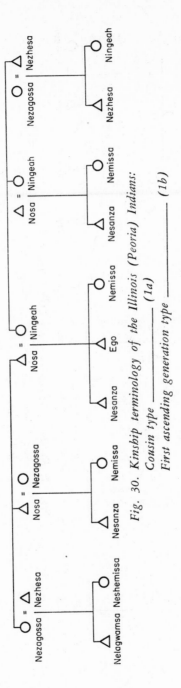

Fig. 30. Kinship terminology of the Illinois (Peoria) Indians:
Cousin type ——— (1a)
First ascending generation type ——— (1b)

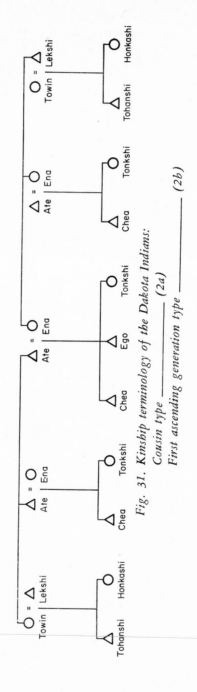

Fig. 31. Kinship terminology of the Dakota Indians:
Cousin type ———— (2a)
First ascending generation type ———— (2b)

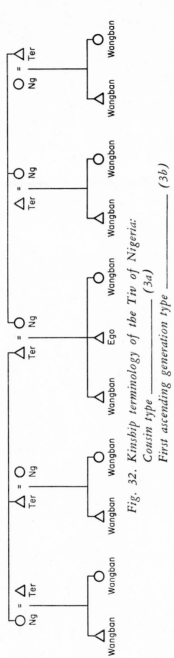

Fig. 32. Kinship terminology of the Tiv of Nigeria:
Cousin type ———— (3a)
First ascending generation type ———— (3b)

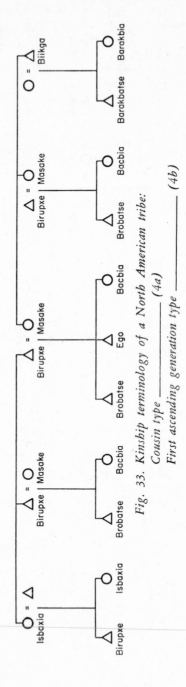

Fig. 33. Kinship terminology of a North American tribe:
Cousin type ———— (4a)
First ascending generation type ———— (4b)

Answers to Figures 30, 31, 32, 33

    1a   Omaha
    1b   Bifurcate merging

    2a   Iroquois
    2b   Bifurcate merging

    3a   Hawaiian
    3b   Generational

    4a   Crow*
    4b   Bifurcate merging

* The North American Indian Tribe of Figure 33 is the Crow tribe.

Part Two

A. Collecting Kinship Terms

1. It was emphasized in the preceding chapter that kin terms must be collected from both sexes. In some societies few differences may be found; on the other hand, in some societies terminology is entirely different for men and women.

    In situations of culture change it is also wise to sample both the young and the old. (Elderly women are frequently the best informants.) Culture change often involves a shift in systems without corresponding borrowing of terms. For example, American Indians with a Crow system may keep their word for FaSi but use it only for "aunts," as the Eskimo system diffuses to them from the dominant society.

2. In his fieldwork the ethnographer talks with as many people as he can. These individuals, or informants, are asked about all their relatives, and genealogies are collected for many families. Any one person usually lacks certain relatives. That is, the first informant may not have a MoBr, but the gaps in terminology are filled in as more informants are questioned. This method is most reliable in establishing the kinship system; also, people generally like to talk about their relatives and may be led from a discussion of kinship into many areas of behavior. Moreover, such discussion is useful in learning about all kinds of behavior predicated on kinship. The ethnographer discovers why his informant avoids certain people while he jokes about sex with other people. This method of "entering" a community was first described by W. H. R. Rivers and is now known as the *genealogical method*.

    A genealogy of a Dakota Indian, one of the author's informants, appears in Figure 34. Although this informant may seem to have innumerable relatives (note that his wife's relatives are not even shown), he lacks several significant ones. Because his mother was the only surviving child of her family, ego would not have used terms for MoBr or MoSi. Obviously then, matrilateral parallel and cross-cousins are missing. Moreover, Dakota have different terms for older brother and younger brother. Ego, in this case, happens to be the youngest sibling; therefore, he would not use the "younger brother" term.

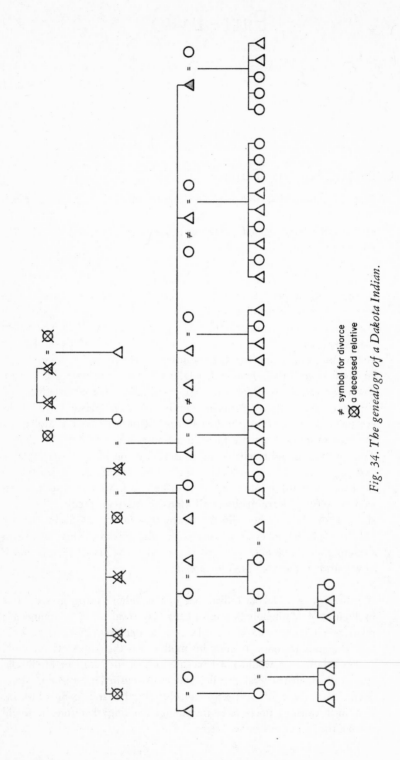

≠ symbol for divorce
⊠ a deceased relative

Fig. 34. The genealogy of a Dakota Indian.

3. Ego, of course, knows the term for younger brother because older brothers use it in speaking to him. He also knows the terms for MoBr and MoSi. Therefore, it is possible to present informants with a hypothetical kinship chart. Morgan, the pioneer of kinship studies, simply used a list of over one hundred items and collected the terms much as one would collect vocabulary. The genealogical method is more reliable than the hypothetical method, especially in societies where kin terminology is changing. Also, it is a much better way of learning about a community. Informants are almost always ready to talk about their actual relatives, either praising or disparaging them, just as Americans do. For very short periods of research, as a check on genealogies, or for work involving only terminology, the hypothetical method is suitable. However, informants vary widely in their ability to understand exactly what the ethnographer wants to know. Some individuals, often the elderly, may understand immediately what is involved in kinship (and even start drawing their own diagrams), whereas other individuals have difficulty in extending terminonology beyond the actual relatives they know.

B. Why Kinship Terms Are Collected

1. The importance of kinship terminology was outlined in the Introduction. For componential analysis the terms in themselves are of value. In most cases, however, the terms are important in that they are a kind of map or model for behavior. The anthropologist centers his attention on human behavior and especially on the interaction between human beings. Insofar as kin terminology is an index to interaction, it is valuable to anthropology. Thus, when an anthropologist says he is interested in how kinship terms change, he primarily means he is interested in how interaction between individuals is changing.
2. At this point it would be well to recall the story of the Australian aborigine who killed a fellow aborigine because the two could find no kinship tie. The example illustrates the point that in the societies that anthropologists study most behavior is regulated by kinship. Anthropologists have become so familiar with some types of this behavior that the types must be learned at an introductory level.

C. Patterned Behavior in Kinship

1. In many kinship systems in many different parts of the world, similar institutionalized behavior is found between relatives. The behavior ranges from a pole of *respect* to one of *joking*.
2. The extreme form of respect is one of *avoidance*. If a Navajo approaches the hogan of his mother-in-law, he makes known his presence so the

mother-in-law may leave. Or he may postpone his visit if he knows his mother-in-law is present. A popular tourist item in the Southwest today is "Navajo" mother-in-law bell earrings. The story told tourists is that older Navajo women wear them so their sons-in-law may leave when they hear the particular tone of their mother-in-law's earrings.

3. A *respect relationship* that does not involve avoidance is possible. The relationship is often found between generations. However, the respect relation is also commonly found between brother and sister, i.e., where there is a sex rather than a generation difference. In fact, the Br = Si respect can even take the extreme form of avoidance. The respect relationship seems to occur between relatives who frequently interact, but who inherently have some conflicting interests.

4. As one moves toward the other pole from respect, *mild joking relations* are found. Generally, more distant relatives are involved but occasionally brothers may be expected to joke with or about each other. Frequently, grandparents and grandchildren are expected to joke with each other, especially when the grandparent is not in a position of authority over grandchildren. In our own society the relationship is one with a lack of restraint; mild teasing and joking may occur. A general respect for age, however, seems to prohibit the institutionalizing of a joking relation so often found in other societies.

5. At the opposite of avoidance is the obligatory joking relation. Radcliffe-Brown describes it as one of "permitted disrespect." The relationship is a friendly one but with occasional implicit hostility. Siblings-in-law are often obligatory joking relatives and the relationship may involve practical and sexual jokes, satire or horseplay. Robert Lowie (1935:28) describes the extreme joking relation among the Crow Indians.

> A man is on terms of the greatest familiarity with his own brother's or clansman's wife. Similarly, he may treat his wife's sister with the utmost license, e.g., raising her dress as to expose her nakedness; and she may jest with him in corresponding fashion. In 1916 I spent a good deal of time in the camp of one informant who was forever fondling and teasing his wife's younger sister, while she returned his treatment in kind. They were not the least embarrassed by the wife's or my presence nor by that of an adult son by a previous marriage of the man's.

6. The reasons for the development of patterned kinship behavior are the same as those behind kinship terminology. However, theories on the institutional factor are particularly well developed and lend insight on the nature of anthropological work in kinship studies. An early analysis of the respect-avoidance behavior was made by Radcliffe-Brown (1952: 109–10).

> The theory that I have offered of joking relationships between persons related through marriage or by kinship is that they occur as

social institutions in structural situations of a certain general kind in which there are two groups, the separateness of which is emphasized, and relations are established indirectly between a person in one group and the members or some of the members of the other. The relationship may be said to be one which expresses and emphasizes both detachment (as belonging to separated groups) and attachment (through the indirect personal relations). These relationships of "friendship," by avoidance or joking, contrast in a marked way with the relationships of solidarity, involving a complex system of obligations, that exist within such a lineage or clan.

7. In a more refined analysis Eggan (1955:79) offers the following hypotheses about types of relationships associated with types of behavior:

    1. Respect relationship—where there is some possibility of conflict and the social necessity for avoiding it.

    2. Mild joking relationship—where there is some possibility of conflict but no particular social necessity for avoiding it.

    3. Avoidance relationship—where the conflict situation is inevitable, where there is the social necessity of avoiding it, and where generation differences are present.

    4. Obligatory joking relationship—where the conflict situation is inevitable, where there is the social necessity of avoiding it, but where no differences of generation are involved.

8. A final note on respect-avoidance relations must emphasize that joking relations are not necessarily symmetrical. That is, a sister's son may have the privilege of joking with his mother's brother, but mother's brother is not allowed to reciprocate such joking.

D. Kinship and Marriage

1. Marriage customs, as well as patterned kin behavior, are closely related to the study of kinship. The sororate and levirate have already been discussed; rules of endogamy and exogamy are likewise based generally on kinship. In our own society the only exogamous rule is marriage outside the nuclear family. In other societies, endogamous rules may encourage or require marriage between parallel or cross-cousins.

2. The anthropologist speaks of correlations between marriage customs and kinship but hesistates to define any causal relation between the two. Therefore, some knowledge of marriage customs is necessary for a student of kinship but it must be emphasized that no implication of a cause and effect relation is meant.

    a. Marriage as a *rite of passage*

    Significant stages in status from birth to death are often referred to as *rites de passage*. Birth, puberty, marriage, and death are almost everywhere marked by societies with social, religious, or political significance. Marriage, as a rite of passage, involves a change in status from single to married person and often is a change from irresponsible youth to responsible adult. Furthermore, it means than an individual acquires a whole new set of relatives and must work out new forms of interaction. Thus, this generally dangerous transition is surrounded by a multitude of norms and supernatural supports.

b. Marriage and children

Marriage in many places is often entered for a *primary purpose* of procreating children. Modern American concepts of marriage differ so much from this attitude that the point must be emphasized. Where individuals are interested primarily in children, a society may practice *trial marriage*. A man and woman live together long enough to find if they can bear children; the couple marry only after a birth.

c. Attitudes toward affines

In many societies the desire for children is coupled with a reluctance to enter marriage. The hesitation seems based on a people's recognizing that affinal relatives are to a degree strangers. The difficulty of acquiring *new* affines is reduced partially through the levirate and sororate or the problem may be resolved in part by marrying a cousin. An uncle and aunt, who are known from birth, become ego's father-in-law and mother-in-law. This practice occurs in cultures from many different parts of the world. Its effects on a kinship system have so many ramifications that cousin marriage is analyzed in a later section.

d. Numbers of spouses

It is common for Americans to feel so strongly about *monogamy* that they consider an individual with multiple spouses as "unnatural." However, we seem unusually interested in *polygamous* systems. Polygamy may be divided into *polygyny* and *polyandry*. In a polygynous system a man has multiple wives; in a polyandrous system a woman has more than one husband. Hollywood offers continual examples of Americans acquiring more than one spouse, but such behavior is labeled *serial monogamy*. Although an individual may have multiple spouses, he can be married to only one at a time.

e. Acquiring a spouse

A common method of acquiring a bride is by purchase. A groom and his relatives compensate the bride's consanguine relatives with a *bride price*. Actually, a woman is not purchased. Generally, the payment should be understood as being the husband's way of bringing his children into his lineage. The bride price functions as insurance that the wife will be well treated. A misunderstanding of this point frustrated many Christian missionaries who found men quite willing to give up purchasing a wife while women bitterly resisted ending "bride purchase." In still other societies *bride service* is practiced. A man works for his father-in-law or the bride's lineage rather than making a payment. Finally, compensation may be achieved through *sister exchange*. "I will give you my sister as a bride if you will give me your sister." Remember that in most kinship systems a man has many classificatory sisters as well as his siblings.

E. Cousin Marriages

1. Sister exchange, if practiced over two or more generations results in the marriage of cousins. Earlier, anthropologists argued that sister exchange *caused* cousin marriage but today's anthropologists are more cautious. All that can be said now is that structurally cousin marrige and sister exchange are connected.

Exercise 17. Diagram sister exchange practiced over three generations.

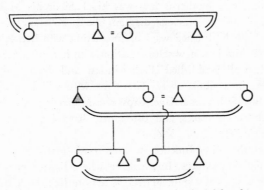

Fig. 35. Possibly your diagram looked like this.

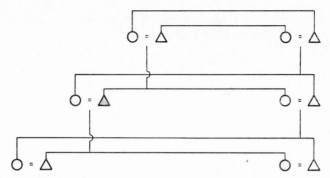

Fig. 36. The diagram can be much less confusing if it is simplified like this.

2. Study Figure 36 carefully. Does ego marry a parallel cousin or a cross-cousin? _____. How was ego related to his mother-in-law before marriage? _____.
How was ego related to his daughter-in-law before marriage? _____
_____. Assume ego is in a patrilineal system. What extra ties does he have to his mother's lineage because of cousin marriage? _____.

3. Where sisters are exchanged (or, from a woman's point of view, brothers are exchanged) in marriage, cross-cousin marriage is the only possible result. Remember that in most systems of terminology the parallel cousins are lumped with siblings and would be ineligible as a spouse anyway. Also, in unilineal societies one set of parallel cousins will always be in the same lineage as ego, and lineages are exogamous. Thus, cousin marriage is almost always of the cross-cousin type. Marriages in the Moslem world are the notable exception; here parallel cousin marriage is frequently found. Murphy and Kasdan (1959) have analyzed and described the structure of parallel cousin marriage.

4. Cross-cousin marriage is generally important in reducing tension between in-laws. Ego's mother-in-law was his FaSi or his MoBrWi before his marriage. In the previous diagram she is both a FaSi and a MoBrWi. From birth he learned ways of interacting with her. Although marriage may put him in a new status relation with her, personal relationships are already well established. Father-in-law and daughter-in-law conflict is reduced in a similar way. The son's wife will be well known to ego from her birth to marriage. Cross-cousin marriage also is a way of firmly uniting two lineages and often may have important consequences in economic life.

5. Perhaps the prime function of cross-cousin marriage is the type of union or fusion it produces. In a culture where lineage principles are strong, society is vertically split. Marriages tend to link the lineages horizontally, but where lineage A marries members of B, C, and so on, the horizontal ties are weak ones. Cross-cousin marriage, however, provides many ties

with one lineage. That is, lineage A members are continually marrying B members. The custom firmly unites two lineages, thus reducing the number of lineage cleavages by half. Like other human groupings, the fusing of A and B or C and D means that the differences between groups A = B and group C = D are increased.

Exercise 18. To understand cross-cousin marriage allying lineages, place a dot in members of ego's lineage, a cross in the lineage of ego's wife. Assume ego is in a patrilineal society.

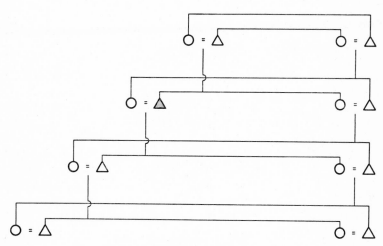

Ex. 18. Diagram for Exercise 18.

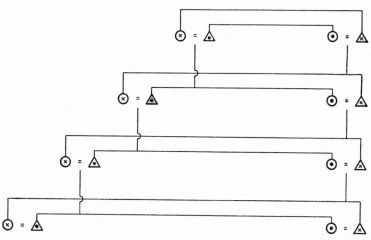

Fig. 37. Correct diagram of Exercise 18.

6. The system diagramed shows *double cross-cousin marriage.* Ego is marrying not only a MoBrDa but also a FaSiDa. In reality such marriage is rare or only ideal. Ego marries any (including classificatory) MoBrDa or FaSiDa. This system is known as *bilateral* cross-cousin marriage. Some cultures prescribe marriage with only *one* of the cross-cousins. When ego must marry a MoBrDa, the system is designated *matrilateral cross-cousin marriage;* marriage with FaSiDa is called *patrilateral cross-cousin marriage.* Of course, a female ego in a *matrilateral* cross-cousin marriage system must marry a *FaSi*So or patrilateral relative.

Although unilateral cross-cousin marriage is rare in societies of the world, it has provoked much discussion because of certain theoretical implications. The factors determining a greater prevalence of matrilateral cross-cousin marriage over patrilateral cross-cousin marriage may be prime factors in other behavior. Thus, the discussion of unilateral cross-cousin marriage is of much importance and has proved to be highly controversial. Homans and Schneider (1955) offered a comprehensive explanation; Eyde and Postal (1961) discussed relevant problems; Needham (1962a) criticized Homans and Schneider at length; while Lane (1962) and Ackerman (1964) have seriously questioned Needham's analysis.

F. Sections and Subsections

1. The potential linkage of marriage ties has been exploited by Australian aborigines in a way which illustrates principles in many kinship systems. It is, therefore, instructive to examine Australian practices. Marriage and family life are used to provide a four-way link. A man of group "W" must marry a woman of group "X"; their children will be members of group "Y" who must marry members of group "Z." These groups have usually been called *sections,* sometimes *classes.* Some Australian groups have compounded the group differences by making subsections, creating eight different groups.

2. For an introduction to the section system, one may assume the existence of four groupings; for simplicity these groups may be called A and B, 1 and 2. Each person belongs to A or B and to 1 or 2. He inherits A or B membership from his father and 1 or 2 membership from his mother. The marriage rules are that a male A1 must marry a B2; their children will be A2's. Descent is thus both patrilineal and matrilineal. Under certain conditions, these rules lead to the formation of what are known as *bilinear kin groups.* Mudock (1949:50–55) provides a full explanation. The male A2 children must marry B1 women; their children will be A1 and belong to the section of their grandfather. The section system is not nearly as complicated as it may seem. A diagram of it reveals its simplicity.

Exercise 19. Indicate section membership for all the unlabeled symbols in the following diagram.

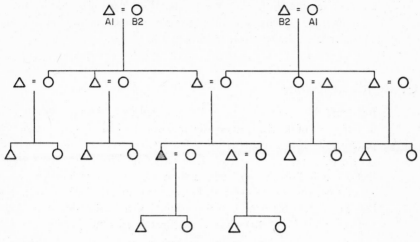

Ex. 19. Diagram for Exercise 19.

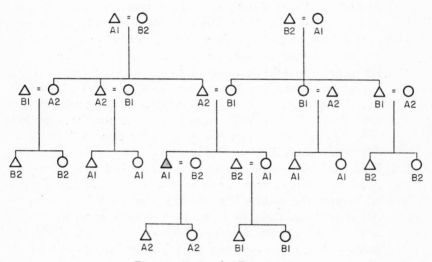

Fig. 38. Answer for Exercise 19.

3. The system is especially appropriate for showing the relation of ego toward parallel cousins as contrasted with cross-cousins. The parallel cousins are in the same class as ego and his siblings, whereas the cross-cousins are in the marriageable section. Notice how ego's sister's children are in a marriageable class in relation to ego's children; that is, they are children of siblings of opposite sex or cross-cousins. One is not surprised to find cross-cousin marriage frequently reported for Australian tribes.

Close examination of the structural effects which differentiate cross- from parallel cousins gives insight into why the former cousins are often a distinct group from the latter. The simple structure of the relationship accounts for the distinction much better than particular marriage customs or other specific behavior formerly assumed to account for the equivalence of parallel cousins with siblings.

G. Residence Groups

1. Residence, like marriage, is closely correlated with kinship systems, and any analysis of kinship necessarily requires detailed study of residence patterns. Residence patterns arise from whatever determines where a couple will live after marriage. In most cultures the norms are specific that a couple "should live" with a certain kin group or independently. A residence pattern can generally be constructed on the basis of the norm but, as in most behavior, actual residence often varies from the ideal. Bohannon (1963:87–90) gives an excellent description of residence rules and practices.

2. In general, newlyweds will select from one of three patterns. If they establish a residence of their own in a new locale, they are said to practice *neolocal residence*. If they live where the groom resides before marriage, they are practicing *patrilocal residence;* if they live where the bride resided before marriage, they are practicing *matrilocal residence*.

3. For several reasons the terms *patrilocal* and *matrilocal* are unsatisfactory; however, they have been in long use and appear frequently in social science literature. Adam (1948) has suggested replacing patrilocal with *virilocal* and matrilocal with *uxorilocal* to connote that the couple lives with a lineage or extended kin group rather than in "father's" or "mother's" household.

4. Residence is also complex because man has devised many alternatives. In some places newlyweds may reside with the husband's male matrilineal kinsmen, the mother's brothers. Such a custom is known as *avunculocal residence*. Cases have also been reported where the married couple do not establish a residence together but continue to live with their own kin, a practice known as *duolocal* residence. Finally, a number of cases are known where the newly married couple establish a residence in one place for the initial years of marriage to be followed by a shift in residence later. Where bride service is customary, a groom may live with his father-in-law while working for him, but permanent residence is established with the groom's patrilineage. Murdock (1957: 670) offered one of the most comprehensive classifications.

5. A further problem in analysis of residence is that everywhere some couples are found who deviate from society's norms. In our own society, for instance, neolocal residence is the norm, but sometimes an

elderly father or mother may live in their son's or daughter's household. The study of individual residence raises a whole new host of possibilities which have been discussed by Alland (1963), Barnes (1960), Bohannan (1957); (1963:86–89), Fischer (1958), Goodenough (1956a), and Murdock (1957).

H. Kin-Based Groups

1. Anthropologists divide the groupings derived from kinship into two types, *unilineal* and *bilateral*. The taxonomy has been criticized by Leach (1961), but the groups remain basic to most analyses of social structure. The bilateral group is less well understood than the unilineal group although anthropologists come from bilateral groups. Pehrson (1954) provided a clear study of bilateral groups; Davenport (1959), Ember (1959) and Solien (1959) made further contributions. The most recent analysis is provided by Goodenough (1962), Scheffler (1962), Blehr (1963), Befu (1963) and Murdock (1964).

2. However, descriptions of *lineages* and unilineal systems still prevail in anthropology, and students must learn a number of details about lineage organization. Technically, a lineage consists of two or more generations of people consanguineously related through one sex. Thus, a man and his children or a woman and her children form a lineage. In some unilineal societies such a group is an operational unit; that is, specific tasks are carried on just by this group. This unit may be called a *minimal lineage*. As lineage membership increases over generations, the grouping may be called a *major segment*. Where major segments are combined because individuals can still trace descent from a single common ancestor, the unit is known as a *maximal lineage*. The use of such classification depends largely upon how people organize themselves. When Meyer Fortes studied the Tallensi of Africa, he found that the people themselves made the distinctions noted above. Since his study, many anthropologists have found the taxonomy heuristic.

3. The lineage is characterized by several features. Regardless of relative size, the lineages within a society are fairly balanced. That is, a lineage of twenty members is regarded as equivalent to one of two hundred members. Each lineage operates as a corporate unit, and its individual members have legal or political status only as members of the group; lineages are therefore often the foundation of political organization.

4. As a corporate group the lineage is also characterized by *perpetuity;* it exists as long as any members survive. Each lineage is charged with certain rights and obligations, with particular duties and offices, and members want to insure that these will not be lost to their lineage. Fortes (1953) explains how perpetuity may be maintained.

5. Another usual lineage characteristic is enforcement of common interest

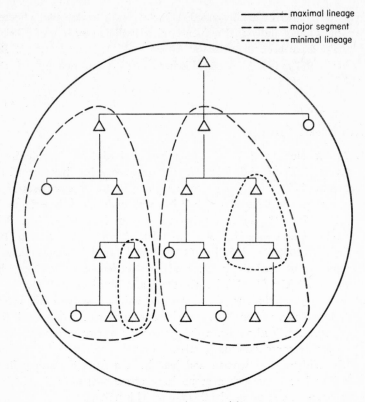

Fig. 39. Diagram of types of lineages.

through religion. Ancestor worship is an obvious form of emphasizing lineage ties, but whatever ritual is involved, it is linked with corporate behavior. Religious and political systems are thus integrated through the lineage structure.

6. Although all unilineal groups have some comman characteristics, certain features differentiate patriliny from matriliny. Schneider (1961) has pointed up a number of differences and discussed their implications. His work cannot be reviewed here, but one example illustrates how descent through females has different consequences from descent through males. Schneider (1961:16) generalizes: *"The institutionalization of very strong, lasting, or intense solidarities between husband and wife is not compatible with the maintenance of matrilineal descent groups.* This is not true for patrilineal descent groups."

I. The Sib

1. The sib has been defined previously as a grouping of two or more lineages. Therefore, the sib is a kin-based group, but the ties of kinship

cannot be traced explicitly. Instead, members of a sib claim some mythological ancestor or otherwise account for common descent.

2. Because of the "feelings" of kinship in the sib, marriage is usually exogamous. Structurally, norms for exogamy are important in order to emphasize the unilineality of the sib. If a person married within a sib, his children would not have the sharp distinctions between paternal and maternal relatives which the sib makes. Lowie's data on the Crow illustrate this point.

> A Crow in such circumstances loses his bearings and perplexes his tribesmen. For he owes specific obligations to his father's relatives and others to his mother's, who are now hopelessly confounded. The sons of his father's (sib) clansmen ought to be his censors; but now the very same persons are his joking relatives and his clansmen! The dilemma affects others as well as himself. (1948:237.)

3. A final note on terminology is essential for the beginning student. The terms *sib* and *clan* sometimes are used interchangeably. British anthropologists regularly use clan for a unit of two or more lineages; American anthropologists are divided about equally in their usage. *Sib* is used in this workbook so that *clan* may be reserved for another unit that is the residential social grouping of sib members and their spouses. For instance, members of a Hopi *sib* are spread throughout the community; male members residing with their wives live away from their family of orientation. In short, the sib is a consanguine group whose common interest is the blood tie. The Hopi *clan,* as defined here, is a group of females and unmarried males related by blood *plus* the spouses of the women. In short, the basis of the clan is *coresidence.*

J. Phratry and Moiety

1. Phratry and moiety organization are based on kinship but are often such large groups that the kin basis is nebulous. Lowie (1948:240) says that the phratry "is evidently nothing but a convenient term for a kin linkage." Briefly, the phratry could be defined as any grouping of *two* or more sibs *provided* there are *three or more* such groups within a society.
2. Where two or more sibs are linked forming only two major groupings, they are called moieties (from French *moitié* meaning *half*).
3. The distinction between moiety and phratry appears pedantic until one reads ethnographic descriptions of moiety organization. When a society is divided into halves, many distinctive features occur which are lacking in societies divided into three or more parts. Lowie (1948) and Murdock (1949) give examples which contrast the features of moiety with phratry organization.

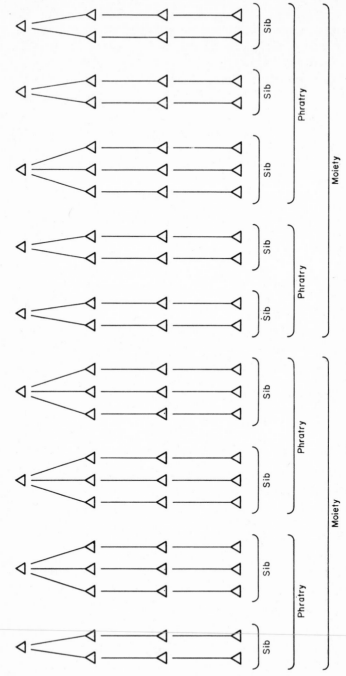

Fig. 40. Illustration of the possible building blocks of a society.

4. The lineage, sib, phratry, and moiety are methods of linking more and more people through kinship. Simply put, the sib is a combination of lineages, the phratry a combination of sibs, and the moiety a combination of sibs and/or phratries. Or a society might be diagramed as in Figure 36, resembling an organization chart of a modern industry or university. Many activities are carried on through the hierarchy pictured below illustrating that organization in a society based on kinship is, in some respects, similar to our own nonkin, impersonal society.

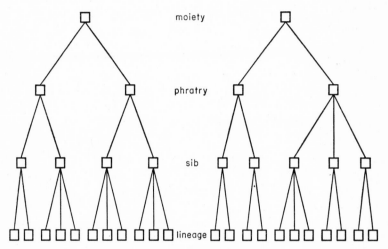

Fig. 41. Organization hierarchy.

K. Review

Part II has introduced more complex forms of organization and definitions have become more difficult. For review purposes the following words should not only be defined but their relationship with one another should be analyzed also.

1. Genealogical method
   Hypothetical kinship schedule
2. Polygyny
   Polyandry
   Serial monogamy
3. Bride price
   Bride service
   Sister exchange
4. Parallel cousin marriage
   Cross-cousin marriage
   Unilateral cross-cousin marriage

5. Virilocal
   Uxorilocal
   Avunculocal
   Duolocal
   Bilocal
6. Corporate group
   Lineage
   Sib
   Clan
   Phratry
   Moiety

Glossary

This glossary of kinship terms has been added to the workbook for several reasons. First, the student may use it while solving problems in the book. A term not fully defined in the text may be further defined in this glossary. Second, the glossary is intended as a dictionary for future use with other sources of material on kinship. Many articles in professional journals assume readers have a wide knowledge of kinship vocabulary. Where this is not the case, a dictionary of kinship terms is most useful.

In addition to serving as a dictionary, one purpose of the glossary is to clarify some terms with different usages. In building this glossary the author was impressed with the consensus that anthropologists have reached for most of their kinship vocabulary. However, because several basic words have been assigned different meanings, literature on kinship is sometimes difficult to follow.

For instance, a "classificatory term" may be defined as a kinship label applied to numerous sets of different relatives. "Aunt" is a classificatory term which classifies together the mother's sister and the father's sister. On the other hand, "classificatory terminology," as defined by L. H. Morgan, is a system which fails to distinguish between lineal and collateral relatives. In this sense the English word "aunt" is part of a descriptive rather than a classificatory system. However, the most famous—or perhaps infamous—word is "clan." Clan has been defined as (1) any unilineal descent group, (2) a matrilineal descent group, and (3) a residential group consisting of the consanguineal members of one sex and their spouses. To add to the confusion, the word "gens" has been used for a patrilineal descent group, and "sib" is often used for any unilineal descent group although the Anglo-Saxon sib was never a lineage. The glossary attempts to supply all the meanings for commonly used terms.

In order to prevent adding to the confusion already present, the author has attempted no definitions of his own. To compile the glossary the work of several leading authorities on kinship was analyzed. From Murdock (1949) came much of the material because his work required explicit definition of kinship vocabulary. In addition, writings of Robert Lowie and A. R. Radcliffe-Brown were analyzed; their definitions have been added when they differed from Murdock's, or when they aided in clarification. Also, works of Fred Eggan, Raymond Firth, Ralph Linton, and others have been consulted in the compilation.

It is hoped that this glossary may be some contribution to a standardizing of kinship definitions. The meanings of many terms have already been standardized; completion of standardization, especially of a few of the most controversial terms, would greatly simplify the teaching of kinship. No doubt, consensus would also reduce controversy in kinship theory because some disagreement is a matter of semantics rather than analysis.

ADDRESS, TERM OF: A kinship term used when speaking *to* or addressing a relative. *See* Reference, Teknonymy.

ADELPHIC POLYANDRY: The marriage of a woman to two or more brothers. It is also called fraternal polyandry.

AFFINAL RELATIVES: Those relatives connected by one or more marital links. *See* Consanguineal, Fictional Kinship.

AGAMY: The lack of any rule in regard to marriage within or without of a group; it denotes absence of marriage regulations on the part of a social unit.

AGNATES: Male or female descendants by *male links* from the same male ancester.

AMITACLAN: A clan with patrilineal descent in which unmarried females reside with a paternal aunt and bring their husbands to the FaSi home. It parallels the avunculaclan, but is only theoretical.

AMITALOCAL RESIDENCE: The norm whereby wives take their husbands to the residence of the bride's father's sister. It parallels avunculocal residence, but is only theoretical.

AMITATE: In the amitate a sister is superior to her brother in that the paternal aunt can dictate the matrimonial destinies of her brother's children.

ASYMMETRICAL CROSS-COUSIN MARRIAGE: *See* Symmetrical Cross-Cousin Marriage.

AVOIDANCE RELATIONSHIPS: A pattern of complete avoidance of speech and physical contact between relatives. Murdock (1949:273) suggests that such a technique is an aspect of sex regulation in societies where sexual prohibitions are not strongly internalized in enculturation; in the same place he briefly summarizes theories of Eggan and Radcliffe-Brown.

AVUNCUCLAN: A matrisib localized around male rather than female members. It is formed through avunculocal residence; that is, males leave their home to live with MoBr and continue to reside there after marriage.

AVUNCULOCAL RESIDENCE: A norm demanding that unmarried males leave their paternal homes to reside with a maternal uncle; upon marriage their wives are brought into the household. (Note that residence is with a MoBr and not a FaBr.)

BIFURCATE COLLATERAL TERMINOLOGY: A system which differentiates the uncles and aunts both from parents and from each other.

BIFURCATE MERGING TERMINOLOGY: A system which groups the Fa and FaBr, and the Mo and MoSi; however, the MoBr and FaSi are denoted by distinct terms.

BILATERAL DESCENT: Links a person with a group of close relatives through both sexes; it limits the number of close relatives by excluding some of both the father's kin group and the mother's kin group.

BILINEAR KIN GROUP. Composed of persons affiliated with one another by both patrilineal and matrilineal ties, including those who stand to one another in such relationships as own siblings, parallel cousins, paternal grandfather and son's child, and maternal grandmother and daughter's child (Murdock 1949:51). In bilinear descent every individual belongs simultaneously to a matrilineal and to a patrilineal group (Lowie 1948: 58).

BILOCAL RESIDENCE: A norm which permits a married couple to live with or near the parents of either spouse; a factor such as relative wealth of the two families is likely to determine where the couple will reside.

BRIDE PRICE: Compensation to parents for the loss of a daughter who leaves her home when she marries; it is commonly a guarantee that the wife will be well treated in her new home.

CLAN: A kind of compromise kin group based on a rule of residence and a rule of descent. It combines a unilocal rule of residence with a consistent unilinear rule of descent and effects a compromise whereby some affinal relatives are included and some consanguineal kinsmen excluded (Murdock 1949:66). The clan is a grouping composed of a number of lineages (Firth 1951:53). Gillin (1948:439) like Murdock defines sibs as two or more lineages united by an assumed ancestor, but he classifies sibs as clans, which are matrilineal sibs, and gentes, which are patrilineal sibs.

Murdock (1949:67) explains the difficulties involved in a definition of clan. "The selection of an appropriate term for compromise kin groups presents the most serious problem of nomenclature encountered in the present work. In the literature they are rarely distinguished from sibs, and the same term is usually applied indiscriminately to both groups. The term most widely used is *clan,* and it is this which we have chosen to adopt after considerable hesitation rather than clutter an already overburdened nomenclature with a new term. There are . . . significant disadvantages in this choice. Foremost . . . is that 'clan' has been used in two other distinct senses. . . . From the time of Morgan until very recently most American anthropologists have used it to distinguish a matrilineal sib in contradistinction to a patrisib for which the term 'gens' has been employed. This usage is now obsolescent, since increasing recognition of the essential similarity of sibs under the two rules of descent renders their terminological distinction no longer necessary. Far more serious is the use of 'clan' by British anthropologists for any unilinear consanguineal kin group of the type which we, following Lowie, have termed the 'sib.' Among recent American anthropologists, 'clan' and 'sib' have run a close race for acceptance in this sense. We have given preference to 'sib' over 'clan' primarily because the former has never been applied to kin groups other than consanguineal ones with unilinear descent, so that its use by us in this sense could lead to no confusion."

CLAN-BARRIO: A clan that resides in a ward of a village or in a hamlet of a community. The community is composed of clan-barrios. *See* Clan-Community.

CLAN-COMMUNITY: One in which a clan is coextensive with a community. All community members belong to the same clan.

CLASSIFICATORY KINSHIP TERMS: Applied to persons of two or more kinship categories; classificatory terms greatly reduce the number of logically possible categories.

CLASSIFICATORY TERMINOLOGY: Partly or wholly blurs the distinction between lineal and collateral relatives. The Hawaiian type of kinship, which ignores differences between father and uncle or brother and cousin, is wholly classificatory. *See* Descriptive Terminology.

COGNATIC KIN: Formerly defined as those related on the mother's side, in contrast with agnatic kin, such kin are now known as "uterine." Cognatic kin are relatives by genealogical ties without particular emphasis on either patrilineal or matrilineal connections. This kind of a grouping has been described as nonunilineal descent, but Murdock (1960:2) feels the term "nonunilineal" is unsatisfactory.

COMPOUND FAMILY: Consists of three or more spouses and their children; it may be produced in monogamous societies by a second marriage giving rise to step-relationships. *See* Extended Family.

CONSANGUINEAL: Those relatives whose every connecting link is one of "blood" or common ancestry.

CORESIDENCE: Local or territorial contiguity. Anthropologists once separated a principle of kinship from one of coresidence by claiming an evolution from the former to the latter; however, ties of coresidence mingle with kinship in establishing solidarity.

CROSS-COUSIN: The child of a father's sister or of a mother's brother; the children of siblings of opposite sex are cross-cousins.

DEME (pronounced "deem"): An endogamous local group lacking unilinear descent.

DERIVATIVE KINSHIP TERM: A term that is a compound of an elementary kin term and another sound or phrase, e.g., "sister-in-law" or "stepson."

DESCENT: A rule of descent affiliates an individual at birth with a group of relatives; this group is intimate and provides certain rights and obligations (Murdock 1949:15). Descent can be patrilineal, matrilineal, or bilateral; occasionally societies may practice double descent, combining patrilineal and matrilineal principles.

DESCENT, MIXED: Gillin (1948:433) notes that mixed descent is relatively rare but two varieties do occur. *Sex-linked* mixed descent affiliates males with their father's male line; females with the mother's female line. *Cross-sex* mixed descent affiliates males with the mother's father, females with the father's mother.

DESCRIPTIVE KINSHIP TERM: A term that combines two or more elementary terms to denote a specific relative. "My brother's wife" is a descriptive term while "sister-in-law" is not. A sister-in-law may be either a WiSi or BrWi.

One must be careful to distinguish between descriptive terminology or systems on the one hand and descriptive terms on the other. Descriptive systems separate lineal from collateral relatives. Thus, "cousin" is a term in a *descriptive system*. However, the term "cousin" may be called a classificatory term because it includes several different types of relatives.

DESCRIPTIVE TERMINOLOGY: Sets off the direct line of a person's descent and the immediate relatives of his own generation from all other individuals. Lineal relatives are all differentiated from collateral relatives.

ELEMENTARY FAMILY: Consist of a man, his wife, and their child or children. A childless couple would not constitute an elementary family. *See* Nuclear Family.

ELEMENTARY KINSHIP TERM: A term that cannot be reduced into component elements. "Father" and "niece" are elementary terms in English.

ENDODEME: The same as a deme. Murdock (1949:64) suggests the word to differentiate it from demes developing exogamy but still lacking a descent rule.

ENDOGAMY: A rule of marriage that requires a person to take a spouse from within the local, kin, status, or other group to which the person belongs.

EXOGAMY: A rule of marriage that requires a person to marry outside such groups.

EXTENDED FAMILY: Composed of two or more nuclear families linked by consanguineal ties. *See* Compound Family.

FAMILY OF ORIENTATION: One in which ego is born and reared; it includes Fa, Mo, and siblings.

FAMILY OF PROCREATION: One that ego forms by marriage. It includes spouse or spouses and children.

FICTIONAL KINSHIP: A socially defined equivalent of affinal or consanguine ties. Adoption, godparenthood, and blood brotherhood are common fictional ties (Keesing 1958:272).

FILIAL WIDOW INHERITANCE: The norm that allows a man to inherit his father's widows as wives, except his own mother. It can occur only in polygynous tribes but even then is rare.

FRATERNAL JOINT FAMILY: Consists of two or more brothers and their wives; the bond of union is consanguineal.

FRATERNAL POLYANDRY: A family consisting of several brothers with one wife in common. *See* Adelphic Polyandry.

GROUP MARRIAGE: A marital union of several men and several women. It probably never occurs as a norm but does appear in exceptional individual instances.

HYPERGAMY: Social class exogamy, i.e., a person must marry into a different social class (Murdock 1949:266).

> Lowie (1948:272) defines hypergamy as a rule that a girl may marry either into her own or higher, but never a lower, caste.

INCEST: Sexual intercourse between two persons who are related by a real, assumed, or artificial bond of kinship that is regarded as a bar to sex relations.

> Where sex relations are forbidden, but not because of kinship, they may be called *mismating*.

> Where either party occupies a status forbidding sex relations, e.g., a nun, sexual intercourse may be termed *status unchastity* (Murdock 1949:261).

JOKING RELATIONSHIP: Patterned behavior between kin that calls for mild to taunting or ribald joking.

KINDRED: A group closely related to ego through both sexes; it furnishes him with certain rights and obligations. Because of the structure of bilaterality, a kindred is never the same for any two persons except siblings.

KIN GROUPS: Any social groupings based on kinship ties.

LEVIRATE: A custom whereby a widow preferably marries a brother of her deceased husband.

LINEAGE: A consanguineal kin group practicing unilinear desent is technically known as a lineage when it includes only persons who can actually trace their relationship to a common ancestor; that is, a lineage is all the unilateral descendants of a known common ancestor or ancestress.

LINEAL TERMINOLOGY: Recognizes collaterality but not bifurcation. FaBr and MoBr are grouped; FaSi and MoSi are grouped; there are separate terms for Mo and Fa. American kinship is lineal.

MATRIARCHATE: Rule of the family by the mother; no strictly matriarchal peoples are known.
"Matripotestal" is a synonym for matriarchal.

MATRICLAN: A residence group of females, the unmarried males of the women's sibs, and the husbands and children of the married females.

MATRIDEME: An exogamous, nonunilinear group with matrilocal residence. *See* Deme.

MATRILINEAL DESCENT: Associates ego with kin consisting exclusively of relatives through females.

MATRILOCAL RESIDENCE: Requires the groom to leave his paternal home and live with his bride, either nearby or in the house of her parents.

MATRIPATRILOCAL RESIDENCE: A pattern of initial matrilocal residence followed by permanent patrilocal residence.

MERGING: The grouping of lineal and collateral kinsmen under one classificatory term. Classifying the FaBr with Fa or MoSi with Mo is a common merging practice.

MOIETY: When a society is divided into two groups so that every person is necessarily a member of one or the other, the dichotomy results in so many distinctive features that a special term, moiety, is applied to them (Murdock 1949:47).
Moieties are half-tribes. If they are exogamous, they are simply major clans. The moiety may be exogamous, endogamous, or agamous (Lowis 1948:240).

MOIETY, COMPOUND AND SIMPLE: Gillin (1948:441) classifies moieties: *simple* moieties are simply large sibs; a society is divided into two parts without component sibs. *Compound* moieties are those which contain sibs and/or phratries.

MONOGAMY: A form of marriage which limits a person to only one spouse at a time. Lowie (1948:114) estimates that few people in history practiced monogamy on principle but that the majority, in fact, led monogamous lives.

NEOLOCAL RESIDENCE: The establishment of an independent household.

NEPOTIC INHERITANCE: The norm that a man inherits his uncle's wife or wives. It has been found in patrilineal groups but fits more logically a matrilineal framework, where it is usually found. It is far from universal with matrilineal descent, however.

NUCLEAR FAMILY: Consists typically of a married man and woman with their offspring. *See* Elementary Family.

PARALLEL COUSINS: The children of a father's brother and a mother's sister are parallel cousins. The children of siblings of the same sex are parallel cousins.

PATRICLAN: A residential group of male sib mates and their wives plus the unmarried females of the sib.

PATRILINEAL DESCENT: Affiliates ego with a group of kinsmen, all of whom are related to him through males.

PATRILOCAL RESIDENCE: Requires the bride to reside with the groom either nearby or in the home of the groom's parents.

PHRATRY: A group of two or more sibs that recognize a purely conventional uilinear bond of kinship (Murdock 1949:47).

> The phratry is a group of two or more sibs united for certain common objects. They may or may not be exogamous (Lowie 1948: 338).

> Note that Murdock claims the tie is kinship-based, and that Lowie maintains the bond is one of common interest.

POLYANDRY: The marriage of one woman to two or more men at the same time.

POLYGAMY: A marriage involving more than two spouses. The polygamous family consists of two or more nuclear families.

POLYGYNY: The marriage of one man to two or more women at the same time.

RAMAGE: A grouping of two or more lineages. Unlike the sib, however, the descent of the lineages is "ambilineal" or "nonunilineal." Descent may be traced through either a male or a female. Firth (1936) uses the term to emphasize the process of fission rather than exogamy. Ramage organization is common in Polynesia and occurs elsewhere in the world.

> Murdock (1960: 11) defines ramages as the functional equivalent of lineages, but, unlike lineages, ego has some choice of membership reckoning descent through either males or females. Like lineages, the ramage group is consanguineal and susceptible to segmentation.

REFERENCE, TERM OF: One used in speaking about a relative. One speaks of a nephew but rarely addresses him as Nephew. *See* Address.

RESPECT RELATIONSHIPS: Behavior patterns between kin that involve standardized ways of showing respect.

SIB: Two or more lineages related by a common, mythical ancestor. *See* Clan.

SISTER EXCHANGE: A mode of contracting marriage whereby a sister or other female relative is exchanged for a wife.

SORORAL POLYGNY: The preferred union of one man with two or more sisters.

SORORATE: A custom whereby a widower preferably marries a sister of his deceased wife.

SYMMETRICAL CROSS-COUSIN MARRIAGE: Marriage with a MoBrDa or FaSiDa. Asymmetrical marriage may be matrilateral, a male ego marrying a MoBrDa; or patrilateral, a male ego marrying a FaSiDa.

TEKNONYMY: A practice whereby a child does not take its name from its parents but rather parents derive a name from their child. For example, an adult is known as "the father of so-and-so."

ULTIMOGENITURE: A rule which favors the youngest-born child in a family; it contrasts with primogeniture.

UNILINEAR DESCENT: The tracing of relationship through either the male or the female line. *See* Descent.

UTERINE RELATIVES: Those kin related to ego through his mother.

UTERINE NEPHEW: Ego's sister's son.

Bibliography

ACKERMAN, CHARLES, 1964, "Structure and Statistics: The Purum Case." *American Anthropologist, 66:* 53–66.

ADAM, LEONHARD, 1948, " 'Virilocal' and 'Uxorilocal.' " *Man,* 48: 12.

ALLAND, ALEXANDER, 1963, "Residence, Domicile, and Descent Groups among the Abron of the Ivory Coast." *Ethnology,* 2: 276–281.

BARNES, J. A., 1960, "Marriage and Residential Continuity." *American Anthropologist,* 62:850–866.

BARNETT, H. G., 1960, *Being a Palauan.* New York: Holt, Rinehart and Winston, Inc.

BEATTIE, JOHN, 1960, *Bunyoro, An African Kingdom.* New York: Holt, Rinehart and Winston, Inc.

BEFU, HARUMI, 1963, "Patrilineal Descent and Personal Kindred in Japan." *American Anthropologist,* 65: 1328–1341.

———, and LEONARD PLOTNICOV, 1962, "Types of Corporate Unilineal Descent Groups." *American Anthropologist,* 64: 313–327.

BLEHR, OTTO, 1963, "Action Groups in a Society with Bilateral Kinship: A Case Study from the Faroe Islands." *Ethnology,* 2: 269–275.

BOHANNAN, PAUL, 1957, "An Alternate Residence Classification." *American Anthropologist,* 59: 126–131.

———, 1963, *Social Anthropology.* New York: Holt, Rinehart and Winston, Inc.

BURLING, ROBBINS, 1963, "Garo Kinship Terms and the Analysis of Meaning." *Ethnology,* 2: 70–85.

———, 1964, "Cognition and Componential Analysis: God's Truth or Hocus-Pocus?" *American Anthropologist,* 66: 20–28.

DAVENPORT, WILLIAM, 1959, "Nonunilinear Descent and Descent Groups." *American Anthropologist,* 61: 557–572.

DESHON, SHIRLEY, 1963, "Compadrazgo on a Henequen Hacienda in Yucatan: A Structural Evaluation," *American Anthropologist,* 65: 574–583.

EGGAN, FRED, 1950, *Social Organization of the Western Pueblos.* Chicago: University of Chicago Press.

———, Ed., 1955, *Social Anthropology of North American Tribes.* Enlarged ed. Chicago: University of Chicago Press.

EMBER, MELVIN, 1959, "The Nonunilinear Descent Groups in Samoa." *American Anthropologist,* 61: 573–577.

EYDE, DAVID, and PAUL POSTAL, 1961, "Avunculocality and Incest: The Development of Unilateral Cross Cousin Marriage and Crow-Omaha Kinship Systems." *American Anthropologist,* 63: 747–771.

FARON, LOUIS, 1962, "Marriage, Residence, and Domestic Group among the Panamanian Choco." *Ethnology,* 1: 13–38.

FATHAUER, GEORGE, 1961, "Trobriand." In *Matrilineal Kinship* (David Schneider and Kathleen Gough, editors). Berkeley: University of California Press.

FIRTH, RAYMOND, 1936, *We, the Tikopia.* London: George Allen & Unwin, Ltd.

———, 1951, *Elements of Social Organization.* London: C. A. Watts & Co., Ltd.

FISCHER, J. L., 1958, "The Classification of Residence in Census." *American Anthropologist,* 60: 508–517.

———, 1964, "Solutions for the Natchez Paradox." *Ethnology,* 3: 53–65.

FORTES, MEYER, 1953, "The Structure of Unilineal Descent Groups." *American Anthropologist,* 55: 17–41.

GALLIN, BERNARD, 1963, "Cousin-Marriage in China." *Ethnology,* 2: 104–108.

GIBBS, JAMES, 1964, "Social Organization." In *Horizons of Anthropology* (Sol Tax, editor). Chicago: Aldine Publishing Co.

GILLIN, JOHN, 1948, *The Ways of Men.* New York: Appleton-Century-Crofts, Inc.

GOLDSCHMIDT, WALTER, 1960, *Exploring the Ways of Mankind.* New York: Holt, Rinehart and Winston, Inc.

GOODENOUGH, WARD H., 1951, *Property, Kin and Community on Truk.* New Haven, Conn.: Yale University Press, Yale University Publications in Anthropology, No. 46.

———, 1956a, "Residence Rules." *Southwestern Journal of Anthropology,* 12: 22–37.

———, 1956b, "Componential Analysis and the Study of Meaning." *Language,* 32: 195–216.

———, 1962, "Kindred and Hamlet in Lakalai, New Britain." *Ethnology,* 1: 5–12.

HOMANS, G. C., and DAVID M. SCHNEIDER, 1955, *Marriage, Authority, and Final Causes.* New York: The Free Press of Glencoe.

KEESING, FELIX, 1958, *Cultural Anthropology.* New York: Holt, Rinehart and Winston, Inc.

LANDAR, HERBERT, 1962, "Fluctuation of Forms in Navaho Kinship Terminology." *American Anthropologist,* 64: 985–1000.

LANE, ROBERT, 1962, "Patrilateral Cross-Cousin Marriage: Structural Analysis and Ethnographic Cases." *Ethnology,* 1: 467–499.

———, and BARBARA LANE, 1959, "On the Development of Dakota-Iroquois and Crow-Omaha Kinship Terminologies." *Southwestern Journal of Anthropology,* 15: 254–265.

LEACH, E. R., 1961, *Rethinking Anthropology*. London: The Athlone Press.

LÉVI-STRAUSS, CLAUDE, 1962, *Totemism*. Boston: The Beacon Press.

———, 1963, *Structural Anthropology*. New York: Basic Books, Inc.

LINTON, RALPH, 1936, *The Study of Man*. New York: Appleton-Century-Crofts, Inc.

LOUNSBURY, FLOYD C., 1956, "A Semantic Analysis of the Pawnee Kinship Usage." *Language*, 32: 158–194.

LOWIE, ROBERT, 1935, *The Crow Indians*. New York: Holt, Rinehart and Winston, Inc.

———, 1948, *Social Organization*. New York: Holt, Rinehart and Winston, Inc.

MALINOWSKI, BRONISLAW, 1960, "A Woman-Centered Family System." In *Exploring the Ways of Mankind* (Walter Goldschmilt, editor). New York: Holt, Rinehart and Winston, Inc.

MATTHEWS, G. H., 1959, "Proto-Siouan Kinship Terminology." *American Anthrologist*, 61: 252–278.

MOORE, SALLY FALK, 1963, "Oblique and Asymmetrical Cross-Cousin Marriage and Crow-Omaha Terminology." *American Anthropologist*, 65: 296–311.

MORGAN, LEWIS H., 1870, *Systems of Consanguinity and Affinity*. Washington, D.C.: Smithsonian Institution Contributions to Knowledge, Vol. 17, No. 218.

MURDOCK, GEORGE P., 1949, *Social Structure*. New York: The Macmillan Company.

———, 1957, "World Ethnographic Sample." *American Anthropologist*, 59: 664–687.

———, 1960, "Cognatic Forms of Social Organization." In *Social Structure in Southeast Asia* (G. Murdock, editor). Chicago: Quadrangle Books.

———, 1964, "The Kindred." *American Anthropologist*, 66: 129–132.

MURPHY, ROBERT, and LEONARD KASDAN, 1959, "The Structure of Parallel Cousin Marriage." *American Anthropologist*, 61: 17–29.

NEEDHAM, RODNEY, 1962a, *Structure and Sentiment*. Chicago: University of Chicago Press.

———, 1962b, "Genealogy and Category in Wikmunkan Society." *Ethnology*, 1: 223–264.

PEHRSON, ROBERT, 1954, "The Lappish Herding Leader: A Structural Analysis." *American Anthropologist*, 56: 1076–1080.

POSPISIL, LEOPOLD, and WILLIAM LAUGHLIN, 1963, "Kinship Terminology and Kindred among the Nunamiut Eskimo." *Ethnology*, 2: 180–189.

RADCLIFFE-BROWN, A. R., 1952, *Structure and Function in Primitive Society*. New York. The Free Press of Glencoe.

———, and DARYLL FORDE, Eds., 1950, *African Systems of Kinship and Marriage*. London: Oxford University Press.

SCHEFFLER, HAROLD, 1962, "Kindred and Kin Groups in Simbo Island Social Structure." *Ethnology*, 1: 135-157.

SCHNEIDER, DAVID, and KATHEEN GOUGH, Eds., 1961, *Matrilineal Kinship.* Berkeley: University of California Press.

———, and GEORGE HOMANS, 1955, "Kinship Terminology and the American Kinship System." *American Anthropologist,* 57: 1194–1208.

SERVICE, ELMAN R., 1962, *Primitive Social Organization.* New York: Random House, Inc.

SOLIEN, NANCIE, 1959, "The Nonunilinear Descent Group in the Caribbean and Central America." *American Anthropologist,* 61: 578–583.

TAX, SOL, 1955a, "Some Problems of Social Organization." In *Social Anthropology of North American Tribes* (Fred Eggan, editor). Enlarged ed. Chicago: University of Chicago Press.

———, 1955b, "From Lafitau to Radcliffe-Brown." In *Social Anthropology of North American Tribes* (Fred Eggan, editor). Enlarged ed. Chicago: University of Chicago Press.

WALLACE, ANTHONY F. C., and JOHN ATKINS, 1960, "The Meaning of Kinship Terms." *American Anthropologist,* 62: 58–80.